THE STORY OF LONDON CHALLENGE

Dedication

This book is dedicated to all those who lead, teach and work in London's schools. It is their effort, energy and commitment that has enabled the transformation of children and young people's achievement and life chances.

In everything we chose to do, we realised we were dependent on the actions, skills and energy of others – principally headteachers and teachers. We had to motivate them to walk countless extra miles, to seek new knowledge, to share generously and to never give up on the belief that their efforts would make a difference, which pupils – and perhaps eventually policy makers – would notice. Teachers can and do 'defeat destiny' in the sense that in individual cases, they can be the influence that overcomes the obstacles created for pupils by poverty and comparative family disadvantage.

Edited by David Woods & Tim Brighouse

The story of London Challenge is published by London Leadership Strategy
Copyright. London Leadership Strategy 2014.
ISBN 978-0-9930720-4-8

"_The greatest danger is not that our aim is too high and we miss it… but that it is too low and we reach it._**"**

Michelangelo.

Other books by David Woods and Tim Brighouse

Brighouse, T.M. and Woods, D.C. (1999)
How To Improve Your School, Continuum.

Brighouse, T.M. and Woods, D.C. (2006)
Inspirations: A Collection Of Commentaries On School Improvement.

Brighouse, T.M. and Woods, D.C. (2008)
What Makes A Good School Now?, Continuum.

Brighouse, T.M. and Woods, D.C. (2008)
London Challenge School Improvement Butterflies, DfES.

Brighouse, T.M. and Woods, D.C. (2013)
The A-Z of School Improvement: Principles and Practice, Bloomsbury.

About the authors

Professor David Woods CBE

David Woods was the lead Education Adviser for London Schools and the London Challenge and then the Chief Advisor until April 2011, as well as being the Principal National Challenge Adviser for England. He was previously Head of the Department for Education and Skills (DfES) Advisory Service and before that the Chief Education Adviser for Birmingham Schools. He is currently the Chair of The London Leadership Strategy and several local authority Education Challenge Boards, as well as being a visiting Professor of Education at Warwick University and a Professorial Fellow at the London Institute of Education.

Professor Sir Tim Brighouse

Tim Brighouse was the first appointed Commissioner for London Schools and then Chief Advisor between 2002 and 2007. He was previously the Chief Education Officer for the city of Birmingham for 10 years and before that Professor of Education at Keele University. Tim spent 10 years as Chief Education Officer for Oxfordshire. He has a national and international reputation as an educational thinker, writer and speaker. Tim was knighted in 2009, for services to education.

Dame Susan John

Sue has been headteacher at Lampton School, a large multi-ethnic mixed school in the centre of Hounslow, since 1997. The school has moved from being a low-performing, unpopular school to a school that is now oversubscribed and has achieved three consecutive outstanding gradings by Ofsted. Sue is also the secondary Director of The London Leadership Strategy and a National Leader of Education. From 2011 to 2014 Sue served as a Non-Executive Director at the DfE. In 2000 Sue was awarded an honorary fellowship from Brunel University and in 2011 was awarded a DBE for services to education. Sue is also Chair of the Brilliant Club Board of Trustees.

Dr Sara Bubb

Sara Bubb served in inner London schools as a primary teacher, subject leader, and local authority adviser. She is now a senior lecturer at the world-leading University College London Institute of Education, where she trains teachers, undertakes research, and supervises Masters and Doctoral students. She played a leading role in developing and implementing the London Chartered Teacher programme and has written widely on teaching and continuous professional development.

Peter White

Peter White is the Primary Director of The London Leadership Strategy. He took on the role of headship 20 years ago and was formerly Head of Brunswick Park Primary School in Southwark. The school has a high proportion of Free School Meals (FSM) children and is resource based for autism. He recently became a National Leader of Education (NLE).

Dr Vanessa Ogden

Vanessa Ogden is Headteacher of Mulberry School for Girls, judged in 2010 and 2013 to be 'outstanding' by Ofsted. Vanessa is also a trustee of Teach First and has been designated a National Leader in Education (NLE) by the National College. Vanessa chairs the board of the Somerset Challenge and is a visiting fellow at the Institute of Education. Vanessa was the President of the Association of Maintained Girls Schools. She won the Women of the Future 'Mentor of the Year Award' in 2014.

Professor Chris Husbands

Chris Husbands is Director of the Institute of Education, University of London (IOE). He was appointed as a Professor and Dean of Faculty at the IOE in 2007, and became Director in January 2011. He led the UK component of the International Alliance of Leading Education Institute's report on Transforming Teacher Education (2008) and on Education And Climate Change (2009). He has written widely on aspects of education policy and on curriculum and teacher development and retains an interest in the teaching and learning of history.

Contents

Introduction   The Story of London Challenge   12
David Woods and Tim Brighouse

Chapter 1   Developing The London Challenge   18
Tim Brighouse

Chapter 2   The London School   32
David Woods

Chapter 3   The London Leader   50
Susan John

Chapter 4   The London Teacher   68
Sara Bubb

Chapter 5   The London Student   88
David Woods and Tim Brighouse

Chapter 6   The London Challenge And Partnership Working   100
David Woods and Tim Brighouse

Chapter 7   The London Challenge – Primary Schools   110
Peter White and Sue Harrison

Chapter 8   The London Challenge: A Regional Model Of School
System Reform And Improvement   118
Vanessa Ogden

Chapter 9   The Legacy Of The London Challenge   132
David Woods and Tim Brighouse

Chapter 10   Lessons From London: What Does The London Challenge
Tell Us About School Improvement And Reform?   142
Chris Husbands

References and Sources   148

THE STORY OF LONDON CHALLENGE

Introduction

The London Challenge and the success of London schools in the past decade has been extensively researched and evaluated. There seems little doubt in what has been written and researched that schools, and pupils within them, have improved their results significantly and that education in London has been transformed. What is in doubt among those writers and researchers, is why such improvement has happened.

Let us first consider that body of opinion and evidence.

There have been two Ofsted inspections – the last one resulting in a detailed report, published in December 2010. The Department for Education (DfE) also commissioned a major evaluation from the London Metropolitan University, published in 2011. The National College has produced several evaluations of The London Leadership Strategy, a major strand of the Challenge. Other reports since the Challenge ended in 2011 included *London Schooling: Lessons from the Capital (Centre Forum)*, *The Mayor's Education Inquiry (2012)* and *The Social Mobility and Child Poverty Commission (2013)*, which highlighted London's success in closing the gaps for disadvantaged children. On a similar theme, there was a key chapter in Ofsted's *Report On Unseen Children (2013)*, drawing attention to the success of London schools in both raising attainment and closing gaps, particularly for disadvantaged children.

The success of London schools and its pupils has proved to be of ongoing interest to researchers and in 2014 alone there were three major reports – *Lessons From London Schools (CfBT)*, *Regional Challenges: A Collaborative Approach To Improving Education (Centre Forum)* and *Doing Them Justice (Institute of Government)*. The consensus of all these evaluations and reports is that the Challenge provided a coherent and robust programme of school improvement; including intensive support for underperforming schools, structural solutions, the use of benchmarked data, school-to-school support and system leadership, and programmes to transform the quality of teaching and learning. The school workforce was mobilised and inspired to step up to the challenge of transforming London schooling. There has also been one attempt to compare the reforming endeavours and their impact in three major cities –Toronto, New York and London – where Fullan and Boyle (*Big-City School Reforms: Lessons from New York, Toronto, and London*) conclude similarly and ascribe the progress, which they rank greater in London than in the other two cities, to a finely judged mixture of what they call 'push' and 'pull' factors.

There have also been several reports, by various economists seeking to find the answer to London's phenomenal success, largely through data studies. This has resulted in some

Evaluations of London Challenge

   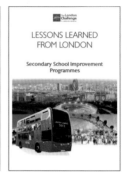

different conclusions – all of them ascribing one or another 'single solution' to the issue of why London has improved. One group has identified the increasing gentrification of London, another the early success of London's primary schools, and yet another the ethnic composition of London's secondary schools.

In their own terms, these single socio-economic explanations raise more questions than they answer. The Simon Burgess research, for example, in ascribing London's exceptional progress to pupils' ethnicity, fails to explain why Leicester or Bradford – to take two examples among many places with strong ethnic diversity – fail to have made progress similar to London. Nor does it address the extraordinary success of Bangladeshi heritage children in Tower Hamlets when compared to Bangladeshi heritage children elsewhere. Other possible socio-economic factors are ignored, such as the ethnic mix of the teachers, who presumably, play some part in the process, though the researchers favouring one solution don't acknowledge this aside from implying that the quality of teaching is a constant in all contexts.

We would argue, however, that the significant improvement in London schools cannot be explained wholly or even mainly in terms of any socio-economic advantages that London may have over the rest of England. We think that it is more complex than that. Theoretically we are encouraged to think we might be right by Nancy Cartwright and Jeremy Hardie's *Evidence Based Policy: A Practical Guide To Doing It Better*, which emphasises the factors at play when policy is successful in one context, then fails in another. In the first chapter, one of us reflects on the assumptions made at the start of the London Challenge on issues similar to those raised by Cartwright and Hardie.

We are both former Chief Advisers for London Schools and as such we have sought to tell the story of the London Challenge as it appeared to those who were there and doing the work. We have all given evidence to the writers of some of the research, to Ofsted and to the various Think Tanks and commentators who have sought to explain the success of London schools. But until now we have not told the story as we saw it. The 'we' are the contributors to this book – ourselves as policy influencers and implementers, school leaders and academics who ran major elements of the programme. As editors, we would argue that in doing this we capture authentic voices of some of the main participants. Some might be regarded as witness statements and we have not sought, therefore, to eliminate some repetition of particular issues because we acknowledge that different participants will have different perceptions of what happened and why it happened.

As this is the story of those that shaped and implemented the London Challenge, rather than an academic evaluation, we have consistently restricted the use of footnotes and references, in favour of a more powerful narrative. There is, however, a comprehensive bibliography at the end of the book for reference. We have also included a selection of quotations and illustrations from many London Challenge publications, to further capture some of the characteristics of the Challenge.

In conclusion, Chris Husbands, the Director of the London Institute, has written an overview concerning the place of London Challenge in the story of school improvement generally and its implications for future policy.

The book starts with the assumptions of one of us when we took on the role originally. We cannot overemphasise the importance we attached to communication and language to reinforce a sense of shared values and purpose. We could not do everything so we had to choose the elements of school improvement on which we should focus. Moreover, in everything we chose to do, we realised we were dependent on the actions, skills and energy of others – principally headteachers and teachers. We had to motivate them to walk countless extra miles, to seek new knowledge, to share generously and never to give up on the belief that their efforts would make a difference which pupils – and perhaps eventually policy makers – would notice. Teachers can and do 'defeat destiny' in the sense that in individual cases, they can be the influence which overcomes the obstacles created for pupils by poverty and comparative family disadvantage. The London Challenge set out to create a 'teacher' and 'school' effect, which would be seen to impact. The metrics others have used suggest that happened on a considerable scale.

Here, some of those who believed it would happen, set out their story.

The chapters can be read independently of each other, giving insights into the work of particular groups such as policy makers, Challenge Advisers, Local Authorities, consultant heads and system leaders and leading teachers, or as part of a continuous narrative of educational reform. There are also illustrations and quotations to exemplify particular aspects of the Challenge.

Educational historians of the future will continue to debate the organisation, methodology and impact of the London Challenge, which as we write continues to sustain performance in London as the best performing region in the country. This book aims to add the immediate policy and practitioner voice to that debate.

Tim Brighouse and David Woods – January 2015

Our DNA

- A compelling and inclusive moral purpose and moral capital with strong, shared values, principles and beliefs.

- System leadership through expert school leaders designing strategies and brokering solutions as well as directly supporting other schools in strengthening leadership and teaching.

- An unrelenting focus on raising standards and closing gaps between groups of schools and pupils so that all children and young people achieve their potential.

- Collaboration, partnership working and practitioner networks sharing best practice through a range of activities, programmes and publications.

- Well mobilised intellectual, social and organisational capital maintaining vision, energy, depth and staying power to produce excellent educational outcomes.

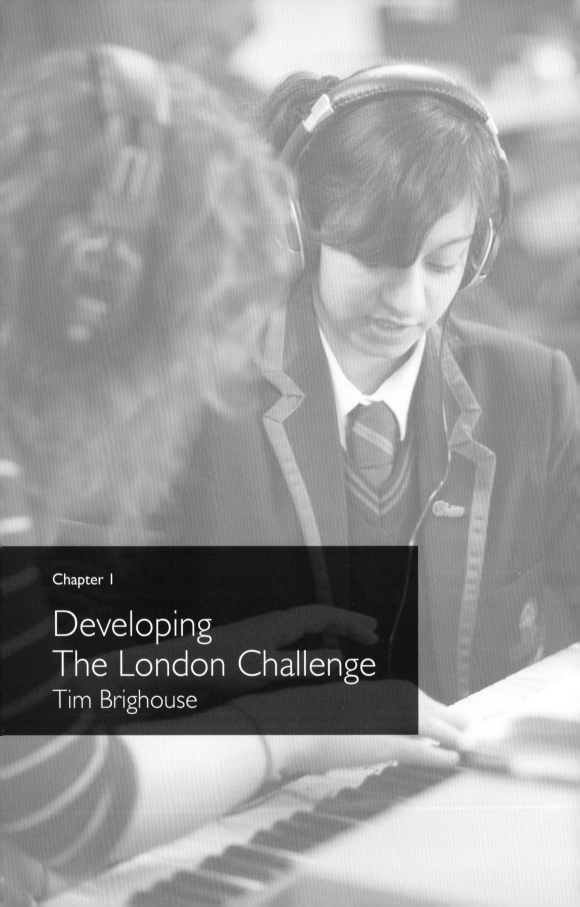

Chapter 1

Developing
The London Challenge
Tim Brighouse

In essence, the London Challenge involved an exercise in bringing about change for the better in a very loosely organised schooling system. At its heart was a 'culture change' at various levels, but principally in schools and their classrooms and in at least part of the Department for Education and Skills (DfES), which was funding and orchestrating the change.

To be successful, complex cultural change of this sort needs to be underpinned by a grasp of three elements. First, to be successful any intervention needs to allow for *differences in context*. What will work in one place – whether school or city – will need to be tweaked to work in another. That requires a deep understanding of what the key differences are and how to allow for them. Secondly, it is helpful to have a *shared map and language*, in this case of 'school improvement', so that there is less chance of misunderstanding when people are trying to learn from each other in order to improve their practice. Thirdly, there is the need to recognise that change often falters because of failure in *communication*, which is the hardest part of leadership and management in any organisation, especially one in the case of the London Challenge, which at the start involved more than 400 secondary schools and 32 boroughs, the DfES and of course a whole set of separate stakeholders such as politicians, headteachers, teachers, support staff, governors, civil servants, pupils/students and their parents. To this array must be added the organisations which represent or act as the gatekeepers to some of these groups such as the teacher unions, the dioceses, employer groups and a whole range of other agencies which could and do contribute to school success – including universities, employers, the churches and faith groups – and an array of organisations in the rich world of the arts. It is small wonder that communication looms large as a perennial issue for improvement. Any leader of complex change, especially complex cultural change, has to calmly accept that communication will fail from time to time and that it needs constant attention.

In the London Challenge, we thought long and hard about these three elements of change. But we also recognised a fourth element of successful change, namely the need to get the right people in the right place doing the right things at the right time. This last factor would affect the running of all aspects of the Challenge, including of course, vitally, schools themselves.

In what follows, I speculate about these four elements, which underpinned the culture change and led to the apparent and unusual success which others say has come from the London Challenge.

First, however, it will be helpful to describe the background to the creation of the London Challenge and how I came to be involved in it.

The then Secretary of State, Estelle Morris, first suggested some special initiative for London in early 2002 when a civil servant pointed out to her that 13% of secondary-aged children living in the capital attended private schools, whereas the comparable figure for the nation was 7%. This factor tipped ministerial thinking, which was already concerned that there seemed to be a general consensus among politicians and journalists that London schools, particularly secondary schools, were places to be avoided if you wanted a good education for your children. This feeling was nothing new and over the years had been reinforced by real and exaggerated stories of school failures and scandals reported in newspapers, especially *The Evening Standard,* which is read by most commuters. London also suffers from the national press being located there and journalists' finding it convenient to illustrate issues by finding London cases to back them up. And bad news sells newspapers.

This negative perception of London schools was well entrenched. It had been the case at least since the 1960s and '70s when first Michael Duane's progressive methods at Risinghill Comprehensive School commenced and then the approaches to schooling at William Tyndale Primary School, both of which led to widely reported school failure and had contributed to a lasting impression that it was difficult to find a good state school, especially a good secondary school, in the capital. Extant statistics showed that at age 16 in 1989 in inner London secondary schools, less than 9% achieved five or more higher grades at GCSE compared with 17% nationally. It is important to mark this figure, although of course there is no reliable way of measuring *overall* standards over time; there is if you wish to measure the progress of different areas of the country by comparing their performance with each other and with national averages, since all will have been affected by any change in measured outcomes of standards over time.

Estelle Morris, who was the MP for Yardley in Birmingham and a former teacher in inner city Coventry, was conscious of general perceptions of schooling in the capital and felt that some focussed effort on London secondary schools would pay dividends. She first secured the agreement of the Prime Minister, whose own difficulties in securing a London state school secondary school place for his eldest son, had attracted some adverse attention: he probably therefore needed very little persuading that her idea was a good one. As Minister for Schools under David Blunkett, Estelle Morris had already played an influential part in the 'Excellence in Cities' initiative launched in 1998. Blunkett and Morris's interest in special policies and resources focus on the inner city had therefore preceded the London initiative. Moreover, as Chief Education Officer in Birmingham I had been closely connected with their growing interest, first in the run-up to the 1997 election and then as a member of the Standards Task Force and as adviser to the 'Excellence in Cities' initiative. In short, I knew that they wanted me involved in London. They claimed – at least to me – that they were influenced in making national policy by what they perceived as the apparent success of policies and practices in Birmingham – and in particular by our approach to school improvement.

At her 50th birthday party at which I was a guest, Estelle, knowing that I intended to retire from Birmingham, sounded me out about my possible interest in heading the London Challenge as Commissioner for London Schools, a post for which I would need to apply through the proper processes. It was plain both that she would welcome an application and that it would be up to me to persuade the interviewing panel that I could do the job. After 10 years in Birmingham, I needed to be satisfied that I had the energy left to do what was going to be a challenging job. In the event I applied and after a set of tough interviews, I was delighted and somewhat surprised to be offered the post, but dismayed that the next day Estelle resigned as Secretary of State. After checking that her successor, Charles Clarke, was comfortable with my taking on the role, I started work at the end of October 2002.

The civil service was well prepared for running the London Challenge. A small unit of five 'fast track' young staff led by Jon Coles had already begun work on how to spend and organise the budget earmarked for the Challenge. Jon Coles was outstanding among his generation of civil servants: a Cambridge maths graduate who had trained to be a teacher, he knew his way around the Department and was widely respected. His analysis of the data and the socio-economic background of London, together with a mutually agreed approach to school improvement across all the capital's secondary schools, formed the basis of what was to become the prospectus for the London Challenge. By the time it was officially launched in April 2003 by the Prime Minister at The Globe Theatre, it had gone through many iterations and much work had already begun.

Jon Coles believed that whatever ministers could afford as extra for the London Challenge should, where possible, be aligned with the existing national programmes and strategies to support our efforts. Two examples of that were the 'Gifted and Talented' programme and the work of the National College for School Leadership. In the case of the former, schools were familiar with the initiative and it was possible to craft whatever we did as an extra for the greater success of what was going on already in schools. In the latter case, the College was under new leadership, Steve Munby a person whom I respected enormously for the work he had done in various local authorities. It was easy to agree a particular approach to their work in London. It was to be characterised by the then novel idea of 'school-to-school' support through consultant heads.

In the six months prior to the official launch, Coles and I had long discussions about how I had approached my job as Chief Education Officer in Birmingham and how it would need to be modified for London. In Birmingham, there was strong local media and given the slightly different role of an officer such as myself vis-à-vis politicians, it was the case that I had a strong 'media-presence' in the West Midlands which it would be folly to replicate in London. My audience, which had been school staff, parents and city councillors in Birmingham, would now be principally school staff. Government Ministers would take care of parents and the local politicians in the 32 London boroughs. So I would write in the educational media and talk to teachers, but not accept the temptation to react in the media – well, not too often!

The goal was the same in both Birmingham and London, namely to inspire heads and teachers that improvement was not just possible but a moral imperative, if in education we saw ourselves as committed to social justice. In my experience, most teachers, while they would not overtly talk in such terms, will acknowledge that as one of the main reasons why they continue to teach. Of course, simply to emphasise the moral purpose of education would not be enough – indeed it could be counterproductive if they thought that the person saying it was not someone they could respect. The fact that I had worked as one of Peter Newsam's three deputy education officers in the Inner London Education Authority (ILEA) in the mid-1970s meant that many of the present generation of London school leaders remembered me, from earlier in their careers, as someone who might understand London – almost 'one of them'. I knew too, that through the unofficial and informal networks of teacher unions and random personal links, what others had achieved in Birmingham while I had been there for the previous 10 years, would also be known in schools.

The principal tasks in both cities were to harness teachers' moral purpose: to emphasise relentlessly 'improvement on previous best' as the mantra underpinning successful children's learning, and as the best means of charting school progress, and to share insights into school improvement and the subtleties of great teaching and learning.

But there were some initial inherited disadvantages, too.

My post had already been dubbed in the press as a 'tsar'. Neither that imagery nor that of 'Commissioner' seemed appropriate if my main task was to motivate teachers. We soon agreed it better to name me as Chief Adviser to London Schools. There was also the delicate question of where I should be located.

After some discussion, I declared my base to be in a tiny shared room at the Institute of Education (IOE) in Bedford Way, rather than the room earmarked for, but not used by me in the DfE. This was to signal two things, firstly that I was not in the pocket of ministers or civil servants and therefore could be seen by the schools to be an independent professional voice, and secondly to be part of the IOE itself – an engine room for teachers' initial training and professional development as well as a world-renowned centre for research. So I saw being a Visiting Professor at IOE as not just an honour, but as an important aid to my role in the London Challenge.

As we put the prospectus together, I argued strongly that there needed to be a change in language. It was vital to realise in everything we said, wrote or did that we were conveying an impression, either positive or negative, to staff in schools on whom we relied entirely to achieve anything. If we could energise and upskill them even marginally, improvement would happen. To keep talking of 'zero tolerance' of 'failure' was to emphasise the wrong thing. Successful teachers know that when they are successful with a pupil's failure to learn, they use three parts of 'appreciative enquiry' – genuinely assessed of course – for every one part of 'problem solving' in feedback to pupils. The same is true of adults. The New Labour mantra of 'challenge and support' needed to be inverted. I was all for challenge but more in the spirit of speculative questioning in the context of being supportive of what schools were doing. It isn't that you shouldn't confront failure – of course you should, but surely in the context of giving those in schools, at least initially, the benefit of the doubt? You should assume they start from the position of wanting to succeed. 'Name and shame' should be replaced by 'no blame' – at least in public.

In the final prospectus there are two examples, one illustrating this change of emphasis and another failing to do so. First, there was a group of schools across London whose headline results on five or more, higher grade GCSEs were unacceptably low. Many of these schools were in a 'special measures' Ofsted category. To call them 'failing', or in conversation refer to them as 'sink' schools, as was happening, would be unlikely to give them the energy to improve. It was arguable that they were in fact 'keys to the success' of the London Challenge since if they could succeed, given the challenges they faced, including being at the bottom of the pecking order when it came to parental preference, then any school could and should succeed. They needed and deserved our support based on the initial assumption that they had within them most of the capacity to improve, if they were given extra well-targeted support. So they were to be referred to as 'Keys to Success' schools and, as such, represented an example of something important but easily overlooked as part of the success of the London Challenge.

Not so the five London boroughs whose overall headline figures were unacceptable. Despite my arguments to the contrary, they were labelled 'failing boroughs', presumably because the principal audience in that category was politicians, rather than schools. Nevertheless I shall not forget the discomfort I felt at the launch in meeting the eyes of their Chief Officers. For me it was a minor defeat.

Another compromise was to accept that the Government was not ready to tackle the unfairness created by the ragbag of individually differing school admission policies and practices, as well as what I saw as the absence of a pan London plan for secondary school places. Instead I had to accept what I regarded as a 'running score' of unfair and unnecessarily imperfect admission arrangements and the fact that Number 10 was determined to build new academies wherever they could find sites, especially if those sites were in inner London boroughs.

I had highlighted these structural weaknesses in the system at the Caroline Benn/Brian Simon annual memorial lecture delivered at the Institute of Education prior to me applying for the job. In colourful language I had pointed out that those from the most challenged urban areas and backgrounds were being entrenched in that disadvantage by a system that encouraged competition among autonomous schools playing fast and loose with admission systems and seeking, not unnaturally, to improve their perceived position in the pecking order of schools, reinforced by league tables and Ofsted inspection categories. In short, I wanted at least some changes to the system to avoid a 'nightmare' scenario of sink schools developing at the bottom end and preferred a 'dream' outcome of all schools co-operating with one another in partnerships with a range of purposes, even to the point where pupils would identify with the overarching partnership, as well as with their school. Although I had made sure that ministers and civil servants had read this paper, which made other trenchant criticism of the direction of urban secondary schooling if prevailing orthodoxies of policy were to continue without some modification, I knew I had to accept that I was unlikely to achieve the structural changes I was advocating.

My consolation was that neither of the issues, admissions and the planning of school places, was a 'fatal wound' to the success of the London Challenge since they were not burning concerns to teachers in individual schools, and it was their actions which would have the most effect on whether the London Challenge was successful. Nevertheless they acted – and continue to act – as a brake on what can be achieved, especially for those gaining least from urban schools.

In those first six months before the launch of the prospectus we were busy putting in place people and habits of working which were crucial to the success of the Challenge. In the fourth element, for example – of getting the right people in the right place doing the right things at the right time – we appointed half a dozen part-time advisers to work with the Keys to Success schools. I later came to refer to them affectionately as our gnarled advisers. Each could point to long and successful experience in schools. An essential common factor in their approach was that they recognised that there was more than one way to lead schools successfully and that the context of time, place and people was a key determinant

Mapping the London Challenge

Effective partnership and networking

Shared vision, purpose and objectives

Challenge and support systems/keys to success schools

Making full use of the data

LONDON CHALLENGE

Close attention to narrowing gaps

Close attention to narrowing gaps

Strong accountability

System leadership and school-to-school support

A relentless focus on teaching and learning

in how to go about things and what to do in any particular school. The, at first informal, and then more formal leader of this group was David Woods, with whom I had worked in Birmingham where he was Chief Adviser before he had taken up a role at the DfES with Michael Barber at the Standards Unit.

This group of advisers would meet weekly, sometimes fortnightly, along with Jon Coles and some of his small team, where we discussed progress of individual schools and 'school improvement' more generally. It was there that we would share what I have referred to earlier as the second element essential to 'cultural change', namely to establish *a shared language and map*, in this case of school improvement. For me, it was learning ever more about seven processes which are the everyday life of schools, namely *leading* creatively, *managing* effectively, *reviewing* creatively, *developing staff* imaginatively, *creating an environment* fit for learning, *involving parents and the community*; and of course, first and last, *teaching, learning* and *assessing*.

Backing these processes was the use of a statistical device we had used to promote school improvement in Birmingham. It had been created there by the statistician John Hill. Schools were put into 'families' according to the socio-economic background of their pupils. Then all the schools in the family were compared on a graph with the vertical being rate of improvement and the horizontal points per pupils, with the intersect representing the average for the whole family. So a school would be in one of four quadrants – low rate of improvement and low points per pupil; high rate of improvement and low points per pupil, high rate of improvement and high points per pupil, or low rate of improvement and high points per pupil. To be really useful, the figures used should be three-year rolling averages. Then all the results in all subjects in all schools are shown. The hope was that schools would be prompted to visit apparently similar schools achieving very different results both overall and in individual subjects.

It was interesting that in Birmingham and in London there was an initial reluctance to use the data in this way for fear of heads objecting that it would create adverse publicity. It was my view such reservations were misplaced since the media were sated with data. In both cities that proved to be the case and a device was created which, in the hands of creative heads hungry for improvement, could prove an invaluable aid.

The adviser meetings (and our discussions in schools) were focused on learning and speculating about the subtleties of the school improvement processes often backed by the Family of Schools database to suggest some 'school-to-school' learning. We would find and share examples of interesting practice. A headteacher reference group was also established to provide reflections and ideas.

I wanted to promote the excitement and energy which would arise from professionals sharing ideas, not burdened by being yoked in a team ploughing ever onward to a predetermined destination. If we were to get better, all of us would be learning and the shared language would aid the speed at which we improved. One of the factors we enjoyed sharing was the collection of what we called 'butterflies', drawn from that part of chaos theory which argued that if sufficient butterflies whirr their wings in the Amazonian rainforest, a thunderbolt might eventually shoot across the United States – i.e. very small actions in a micro-climate can have great impact further away or more generally. We thought there were practices in schools which required little effort but could have great impact. Schools related to that idea, just as they had in Birmingham. So we set about collecting ideas, sharing them and eventually publishing collections of 'butterflies'. All this was intended to contribute to cultural change.

My personal habit would be to get up early to visit schools. I travelled by tube and train to arrive as children and staff were arriving – often a good opportunity to form an impression of the atmosphere and relationships between staff and pupils. I tried to ask questions and keep conversations both positive (about teaching and school practices), open-ended and speculative. I always followed up with handwritten letters to all the staff I met, trying to be careful to convey messages to individual staff that would be accurate and positive but not undermine the messages the school leadership was wishing to reinforce. As many as 20 letters or more per school would be written in this way and I visited almost 100 schools in that six months. Choice of school was mainly dictated by travel routes and I therefore found myself in a whole range of differently performing schools. Once the gnarled advisers were at work I would only visit Keys to Success schools at their request, or with their agreement determined at our weekly meetings.

Many evenings in the first year of the London Challenge would be spent over meals with small groups of key people who might want to move some of our agendas forward. It was in this way, for example, that the Southwark Schools Partnership which straddled the state/private divide was founded. It was to last involving many thousands of pupils in shared learning and hundreds of teachers in professional development activity. But there were other equally fruitful evenings involving music and the arts and a range of school improvement possibilities with mostly educational leaders in London. More than one of these evenings was devoted to fleshing out the National College's role and the implementation, overseen by the seconded head Alan Davison and later George Berwick, of the consultant head, 'school-to-school' support programme of what came to be known as The London Leadership Strategy.

Overcoming the autonomy, which can so easily lead to independent isolation of schools, was one of the changes in culture I was seeking to secure. The London Leadership Strategy, coupled with the use of the Family of Schools database were keys to turning that intention into reality.

There was an easy, trusting and relaxed relationship among Stephen Twigg, the minister charged with overseeing the London Challenge for the Secretary of State, Jon Coles and myself. We consciously shared out who had lead responsibility for making sure certain things happened and met as a trio to take stock on a weekly basis, although we met each other more frequently in the course of business.[2]

In the early days of the London Challenge therefore, a changed climate was being set. We were quite simply looking to create a climate in which the 'energy creators' could flourish and the 'energy consumers' would find as little as possible fuel to fan their discontent.

The four elements outlined at the beginning of this chapter had been thought about. We were paying careful attention to context both in schools and in the part of the DfES which ran the Challenge (and for me some key differences between London and Birmingham). I would have what we called 'greasy spoon' breakfasts with Jon Bangs and some of his colleagues at NUT, for example, and other similarly informal meetings with other teacher union leaders. It was important that they were comfortable with what we were doing.

Jon Coles regularly attended the monthly meetings of the Chief Education Officers of the London Boroughs and enabled some inter borough initiatives around key issues. It was very important that we didn't cut across their own school improvement efforts with schools.

We had established the use of different language which would reflect, support and challenge and we had established a theoretical map and language to be shared in school improvement and we were paying attention to communication to key stakeholders. One of the subtleties of leadership in very large organisations especially one so loosely coupled as the London Challenge, is to realise that you are a 'remote' leader. That requires a very different approach from leadership which involves day to day contact with those you lead.

Finally, we had arranged for some key people to be in the right place, doing the right things at the right time.

Cultural change of this sort, however, is also complex change. One of the helpful ways of looking at this is set out in the following diagram:

Managing Complex Change

Vision	+	Skills	+	Incentives	+	Resources	+	Acton Plan	=	Change
	+	Skills	+	Incentives	+	Resources	+	Acton Plan	=	Confusion
Vision	+		+	Incentives	+	Resources	+	Acton Plan	=	Anxiety
Vision	+	Skills	+		+	Resources	+	Acton Plan	=	Resistance
Vision	+	Skills	+	Incentives	+		+	Acton Plan	=	Frustration
Vision	+	Skills	+	Incentives	+	Resources	+		=	Treadmill

Adapted from Knoster, T. (1991) Presentation at TASH Conference, Washington DC

However useful such a diagram is – and it is essential to get all the five factors in place – it will be negated if the elements I have outlined regarding cultural change are not in place.

So we used both in implementing the London Challenge.

The prospectus reveals the underpinning strategy around four themes – the **London School**, the **London Teacher**, the **London (School) Leader** and the **London Student**. You can use the five elements in the above diagram for each of the four themes.

I have elaborated sufficiently our approach to the London School and the London Leader in what I have outlined about cultural change and in doing so have illustrated Knoster's diagram. It is worth elaborating the London Teacher and the London Student.

London has always suffered from comparative teacher shortages, often relying on recruiting young teachers from other countries attracted to spend some time in one of the world's leading capital cities. When we started in 2002 I was struck by that factor as I visited schools. While that is probably a vital lifeline for teachers, we wanted to increase the flow of home-grown new recruits and then retain those we had for marginally more time. So far as the first aim was concerned, my being based at the IOE helped not least because of working links with staff there. But I believe that 'Teach First' – an idea imported from America – was crucial to enhancing the reputation of teaching as a profession which would appeal to the best young graduates. The idea was controversial and not popular, at least at first, with traditional university providers of initial teacher education because it was based on a six-week summer of training followed by mentoring on the job and the job being in the most challenging schools. The theory behind the scheme was that it would be possible to attract high-quality graduates from Russell Group universities to teach for two years before going into business or the city. It was my bet that at least half those recruited in this way would be so fascinated by teaching and schools that they would stay in the profession. In short, if it were successful and although few in number compared with the size of the teaching, it could contribute to a cultural change signifying that it was a reasonable and exciting career choice for good young graduates. So it has turned out.

Jon Coles had other ideas for teachers including working assiduously to gain them favourable housing opportunities in order to help retention, plus an inner London pay scale.

One of my priorities was teachers' professional development. It has been wherever I have worked. Too often policy makers forget the obvious point that it is the quality and skill of the teacher that makes the difference. It has always struck me as odd that Ofsted reports on schools rarely mention the issue of staff development when it is the case that it is a consistent feature of outstanding schools. Teachers' intellectual curiosity always needs to be re-fuelled.

Of course, how you promote it is affected by context and I thought we should do more than simply emphasise its importance as one of the four processes of school improvement. So we floated the idea of the Chartered London Teacher as something for all London teachers to consider. The argument was that to teach in London successfully required a teacher to have more skills and expertise than would be the case in, for example, a mono-cultural affluent suburban school setting. Within the chartered scheme, teachers would provide evidence through visits, observations and practice that they were extending their knowledge of pedagogy, their subject, whole school issues, children's special needs and community issues such as the implications of English as an Additional Language (EAL) among their pupils. In return for doing it, teachers would get £1000. In practice, it took some time to get off the ground but some judicious informal words with the teacher unions ensured it took off. It was to have a short life, as all national initiatives and financial support for teacher CPD do, but it helped change a climate and under the leadership of Sara Bubb at the IOE provided a catalyst for teachers and schools learning from each other.

Finally, there was a fourth theme within the prospectus, the 'London Student', which was meant to be a vehicle for harnessing the enormous 'common wealth' of London to extend the opportunities in the arts, sport and in much else to all students in all schools by seeing them adopt a 'Student Pledge'. Although we did an enormous amount to promote it, we didn't find a way to make it stick to any lasting extent, as we hadn't in a similar scheme in Birmingham a decade earlier. It isn't that nothing happened or that it wasn't important, it is simply that the accountability measures, which focus school attention elsewhere, ignore the issue of transformative experiences for young people which the scheme was trying to promote.

In short, notwithstanding some excellent student initiatives especially around the Gifted and Talented programme, if one were judging the success of the London Challenge, you would give it a lower mark on this aspect, although of course in terms of pupil attainment it was a huge success and that was the main metric for which we were to be held to account.

That raises a final important point. At a time when the government was fascinated by target setting, the London Challenge largely escaped them. Of course, the Number 10 policy unit set some for us but we set most for ourselves. We wanted to get the usual metrics – principally GCSE results at 16 and progress from age 11 – above the national average when it would be possible to claim to politicians that if they thought there was a problem in London, then it must be worse elsewhere. What is more, we thought that a reasonable goal would be that we should be able to show that whatever socio-economic group you looked at, London schools would be doing better. We also wished to increase the percentage of good and outstanding schools, building not only moral purpose, but also moral capital into the system.

Chapter 2

The London School
David Woods

In 2002, the negative perceptions of London's state schools, the secondary schools in particular, were well entrenched with a much higher percentage of pupils attending private schools than anywhere else in the country. Although there were some excellent schools, it was increasingly felt that amongst London's 400 plus secondary schools, there were far too many where educational aspirations and performance were too low. Certainly in terms of attainment, London schools were being outperformed by those in the rest of England. The most urgent task facing the Challenge was to work exceptionally closely with the schools that were failing to reach acceptable standards and to take whatever decisions were necessary to raise the quality of those schools. Therefore, after the formal launch of the London Challenge in April 2003, there was an intense focus on those schools where pupils' achievement was the poorest.

The Keys to Success secondary schools programme

When identifying and working intensely with those schools, the London Schools Commissioner, Tim Brighouse, was determined to change the prevailing government narrative of 'failing', 'underperforming' and 'poor schools in challenging circumstances' to one that established a tone of expectations and optimism that these schools could improve, given the right balance of challenge and support. These schools were therefore badged as 'Keys to Success' schools and allocated a London Challenge Adviser empowered to develop with them bespoke solutions, which would be centrally resourced.

The DfES floor target was then 25% five A-C passes and Contextual Added Value did not exist as a performance measure. The first wave of Keys to Success schools was chosen mainly because they were around or below 25% five A-C or because they were in the then Ofsted categories of serious weaknesses and special measures. There were some 70 of these out of a total of 407 schools organised into a triage system of 'intensive support', 'intermediate' and 'light touch' corresponding to a RAG grading system in terms of school performance. From the outset, the rigorous use of data underpinned working with these schools, identifying and targeting key attainment gaps. Good quality data about families of schools across the city was made available to help all schools, particularly Keys to Success schools, benchmark their performance with schools in similar settings, giving them a further tool for self-improvement and the means to seek out good practice themselves.

Since 2003, the programme developed further and in negotiation with local authorities, successive waves of schools joined the programme having been placed in an Ofsted category or seen their results decline. Others left the programme typically after two or three years having secured an improvement trajectory and built much more of an achievement culture.

The criteria for joining the programme was then much more related to the floor target 30% five A*-C including English and Maths. Between 2003 and 2010, some 110 schools had at some point been in the programme (27% of the London total).

Objectives of the Keys to Success programme

- To break the link between deprivation and underachievement by narrowing attainment gaps between groups of pupils and schools.

- To build a culture of achievement.

- To raise standards with a particular focus on GCSE outcomes and progression from Key Stages 2 to 4.

- To embed best practice in teaching and learning at all levels, aligning with the National Strategies.

- To strengthen schools' ethos and improve parents' and pupils' perceptions.

- To enhance leadership and the capacity of schools to sustain their own improvement.

It was recognised that these objectives could only be met through effective partnerships, working with local authorities (LAs) and their school improvement services, including School Improvement Partners (SIPs), as well as with national agencies for school improvement such as the National Strategies and the National College (The London Leadership Strategy).

Methodology for supporting and challenging Keys to Success Schools

In the summer term, negotiations were held with LAs based on predictions as to what support their schools would need in the next year. Every September, Advisers and the London Challenge team conducted a 'triage' session based on the reported performance data to decide which category of support schools needed or whether they should leave the programme as an 'alumni' school. Schools could change categories during the year if there were new circumstances, e.g. being placed in an Ofsted category. A London Challenge Adviser was allocated to all schools in the 'intensive' category of support to work on a focused programme of improvement, liaising with LA officers and SIPs reporting to ministers through the Civil Service. The Adviser and the London Challenge team could broker and commission support within a set allocation of funding. Similarly, a London Challenge Adviser was allocated to 'improving schools' but schools in the 'improving' category were supported by providing five extra days for SIPs to broker support in conjunction with their LAs. They could contract with the London Challenge's main provider of services, 'Education London', up to a set budget limit. Extra support can be negotiated with the London Challenge Adviser for that school and the advisers themselves provide up to five days' support. Considerable attention was paid to data sets and the use of data within schools, particularly pupil tracking systems leading to personalised intervention strategies focused mainly on raising attainment in English and Maths.

The Challenge appointed two Specialist Advisers, one for EAL and one for behaviour management and whilst their first priority was 'intensive' schools, they also supported 'improving schools'. This support was commissioned through the School's Challenge Adviser and there was a pan London EAL strategy, which provides extra support that can be accessed by all London schools. Advisers brokered and commissioned support based on the schools' needs, performance and priorities, seeking to align this with existing LA support and that from the National Strategies and to help the school make the best use of a range of interventions. The London Challenge appointed a main contractor to provide services (Education London) and support packages were commissioned by the school and the advisers. Other support, such as the supply of Teach First teachers, providing interim senior leadership or dealing with highly specific issues, was brokered directly by the London Challenge Advisers. Where progress was off track, corrective action was taken rapidly to improve performance. Advisers also worked closely with The London Leadership Strategy (under the auspices of the NCSL) and Local or National Leaders of Education were allocated to 'intensive' schools and some 'improving' schools in order to provide a variety of leadership support. Challenge Advisers also brokered LLS programmes, working with the attached school leaders such as the Improving Teacher and Outstanding Teacher programmes, subject specialist support including Advanced Skills Teachers and securing good behaviour.

A further development was the designation of 'London Teaching Schools' (before the official DfES programme), which offered the full range of teaching and learning programmes to Keys to Success schools in specific school settings. Advisers supported collaborative working at a city-wide level, encouraging the practical use of the Families of Schools data and inter-visiting between schools to observe good practice, as well as the adoption of the Chartered London Teacher Scheme. They also supported schools in transition to Federation, Academy and Trust status. In particular circumstances (usually schools in special measures, notice to improve or below the floor target), advisers worked with LAs to set up school improvement boards or their equivalent with representatives from the school, governors, LA, the London Challenge and the SIP meeting every half term to review support and progress. Occasionally, an Interim Executive Board was established, working closely with the LA and Challenge Adviser. The London Challenge model was also used in the other City Challenge areas of Greater Manchester and the Black Country. It was also the model for the work of National Challenge Advisers supporting National Challenge schools between 2008-2010.

Our shared language

The key words for effective London Challenge practice in raising standards and building a lasting culture of attainment and aspiration particularly for Keys to Success schools, were:

Collective AMBITION and ASPIRATION

A proper sense of CHALLENGE at all levels

The importance of the right SUPPORT

The necessity of absolute FOCUS

Using appropriate LEVERAGE to secure solutions

Working at a PACE to make PROGRESS

Ensuring IMPACT

Securing SUSTAINABILITY

Impact of the programme

Standards rose faster in Keys to Success schools than other schools in London and nationally. The average annual improvement rate between 2003-2009 was 5% compared with a national improvement rate of 2.6%. In terms of five A*-C including English and Maths, Keys to Success Schools improved by 7% between 2008-2009 as opposed to the national improvement rate of 2.5%. There was a significant decline in schools in special measures, from 17 in 2003 to three in 2010 and also in 'notice to improve' schools – nine in 2010. Both of these figures were well below national averages. Six schools, which started as Keys to Success schools such as Southfields Academy, under the leadership of Jackie

Figure 3 – Difference between
percentages of schools (primary) judged
'good' or 'outstanding' in London and
England (2000/2003 and 2013)

Figure 4 – Difference between
percentages of schools (secondary)
judged 'good' or 'outstanding' in London
and England (2000/2003 and 2013)

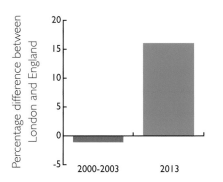

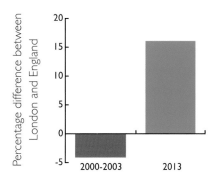

Source: Regional Challenges – A Collaborative Approach
To Improving Education, Centre Forum, RM Publications (2014)

Valin and Lilian Baylis Technology School, under the leadership of Gary Phillips, became 'outstanding' in subsequent years and a considerable number of others became 'good' or 'good with outstanding features'. There were increasing numbers of 'alumni schools' which left the programme with good school improvement trajectories to sustain continuing success and who then helped other schools to succeed. There was a group of schools where the LA and the London Challenge Adviser working with the DfE concluded that the school improvement trajectory was never going to be strong enough and they either closed, federated or became academies. In the Ofsted reports, headteachers were said to like best specialist Adviser support and challenge, consultant headteacher support school-to-school support, and direct funding for school improvement.

Lessons learnt from the Keys to Success programme that could influence school improvement in England were reported by Ofsted as being political leverage through the Minister for London schools and the Chief Adviser for London, also the use of well-respected and experienced expert advisers, good use of data including the Families of Schools, access to a wide range of suitable resources – all working in a challenge and support role with local authorities and their schools. Other commissioned reports from university researchers focused more generally on the leadership strategy in relation to Keys to Success schools. They refer to the role of Consultant Leaders in helping schools to build leadership capacity, strong working partnerships between the London Challenge Adviser, consultant leader and local authority advisers, the successful sharing of expertise across two or more schools, the effectiveness of coaching and mentoring, the direct tackling of barriers to raising achievement and the importance of data analysis, setting priorities and having a clear focus on raising standards.

The London Challenge Adviser

In 2003, London Challenge Advisers were first recruited by the DfES on a part-time consultancy basis to work primarily with Keys to Success secondary schools and related local authorities. In 2008, a primary team of advisers were also recruited led by Anne Berger. Many of these advisers had been successful headteachers themselves before filling key roles as senior local or national advisers, directors and deputy directors of local authority children's services, senior education consultants or Her Majesty's Inspectorate (HMI) such as George Gyte, Victor Burgess and Heather Flint. They were highly credible school improvement experts who knew how to fix problems and to advise on bespoke solutions for individual schools.

This expertise and practical support included successful experience of improving their own and other schools, analytical skills and the necessary expertise with data to examine school performance forensically. Advisors had leadership skills to support and empower senior school leaders to make tough decisions and also to manage such stakeholders as governors and local authorities. Advisers also had knowledge of the strengths of different kinds of training provision in a range of schools, Local Authorities and private contractors that might provide support and a detailed knowledge about the expertise and skills of individual leaders in education who might support the headteachers of a target school.

The Ofsted Report of December 2010 commented that:

'The leadership skills within the London Challenge Adviser team are such that advisers, in almost all cases, can quickly establish effective partnerships with the staff of the supported school... helping schools retaining the sense that they were in control of their own destiny... and that they were genuine partners in the process of school improvement which was being done with them not to them' and that 'The main function of a London Challenge Adviser is to act as a catalyst to bring about swift improvements in underperforming schools'.

Ofsted Report, December, 2010

- To provide professional advice, challenge and support to local authorities in relation to individual schools and school improvement strategy.

- To offer professional advice, challenge and support to underperforming schools.

- To analyse and identify issues impacting on school improvement and broker appropriate support to raise standards and build capacity to sustain improvements.

- To narrow the attainment gap between disadvantaged groups and their peers.

- To represent the London Challenge team and the Department as the front-link between the Department and schools.

- To identify opportunities for the establishment of academies, Trust Schools and Federations and to work with nominated officials in the Office of the Schools Commissioner (OSC).

- To successfully manage relationships with multiple stakeholders and gain their support to deliver against individual school improvement plans.

- To work with other advisers, the City Challenge team and The London Leadership Strategy to provide strategic solutions to help improve school standards.

However, this is only an outline description and it is important to state the very special aspects of this role.

The first aspect connects to the fundamental moral purpose in helping the most challenged schools succeed in raising standards and thereby improving the life chances of many children and young people. Advisers worked to make a real difference to these schools through their passion, conviction and determination to deal with denial if necessary, but also to be resilient and persuasive so that this task could be achieved by all schools with the right support and challenge.

Secondly, Challenge Advisers were so called because they were expected to challenge the status quo whether in schools or local authorities, with the best challenge being the best support, whether it was to the senior leadership of the school or the local authority, in helping to develop the capacity to improve and to build an achievement culture. Of course, challenge is only effective if it leaves the school/local authority in a more energised sate, believing that there are solutions to very difficult issues and that there is a positive and sustainable way forward. Abraham Lincoln once said "he has the right to criticise who has the heart to help" and there can be no place for challenge without intensive, personal commitment and involvement in providing the best support to improve schools.

Thirdly, advisers brought to this role what we call the 'tradecraft' of school improvement – those special skills that enabled them not only to analyse performance data effectively and diagnose key issues, but the clarity and focus to help schools overcome barriers to attainment and the judgement to see what support and interventions would enable the schools to make progress at a pace. They were fast on their feet in devising bespoke solutions and using the most high leverage interventions that would make a real difference. Further, they contributed to the whole London Challenge Adviser team particular specialist knowledge and practice that could be shared and used effectively with all London schools. This could be through deep knowledge of curriculum aspects or teaching and learning, but all Challenge Advisers were highly experienced practitioners with a significant leadership background and proven expertise and experience in school improvement. This enabled them to demonstrate empathy as well as authority and to motivate heads and schools always to improve on their previous best performance.

Fourthly, was the capacity to broker and commission the right support from outside the school, whether this was from Education London in the case of secondary schools, The London Leadership Strategy, the variety of Department for Education programmes that could be accessed effectively, support from specialist advisers in English as an Additional Language (EAL) and behaviour, or bespoke bids for resources that could help to solve a particular problem. Of course, you can overwhelm a school's implementation capacity with too much support and too many extra programmes – and their skill was to help the school align the most effective support to the key priorities. In a sense, this gatekeeping role was as important in seeking the best solutions and working with the school to establish a relentless focus on those strategies that really would make a difference.

The final aspect of the role connects to personal accountability and credibility in working with school leaders, governors and the local authorities to secure robust Raising Attainment Plans and to help make adjustments where necessary, being careful to empower school leaders to make tough decisions. Regular monitoring and reports of progress were essential given the need to drive forward improvement at a pace to secure objectives and also build long-term sustainability. This was done through regular visits to schools, data scrutiny, focused conversations with senior and middle leaders, governors and pupils, attendance at Monitoring Boards and local authority meetings and evaluations through reports and meetings to secure rapid improvement and if necessary, work with the local authority and DfES to broker structural solutions.

The Adviser Team

London Challenge Advisers had a high level of autonomy in operational decision making, which led to the rapid delivery of solutions. The knowledge, skills and experience of individual team members was exceptionally high with high levels of trust in the competence, expertise and integrity of colleagues and professional leadership within the team. There was a shared commitment to operational strategies for the delivery of key outcomes and clear lines of accountability within the team and within the wider operation of the London Challenge.

"The Adviser Team benefited from a 'London-wide awareness of school performance, complete with good evidence-based intervention, irrespective of a school's location, status or circumstances… this awareness also gives credibility and assurance to a school that receives support, because its leadership knows that the London Challenge Leaders have access to a huge range of expertise and practical support'.**"**

Ofsted, 2010

Characteristics of the work of the London Challenge Adviser

Common characteristics distinguish the iterative process that underpins their work. The challenge stages towards improvement are represented in the diagram:

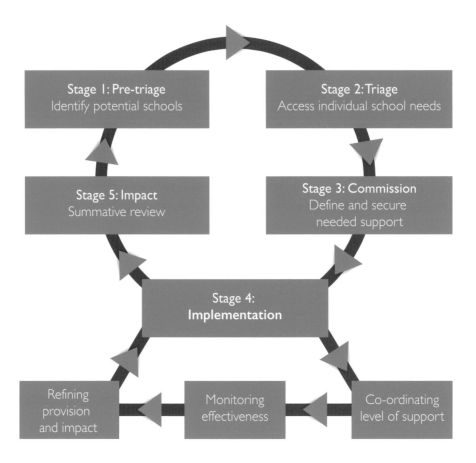

The use of data as a powerful lever for change in London schools

The London Challenge placed the use of performance data at the heart of its programme as a key both to powerful accountability and well-targeted support. It is easy to forget that the use of data in the education system at the beginning of the Challenge in 2003 was extremely limited. In the Challenge, right from the outset, intensive analysis underpinned the framing of the problem and the initial approach and vision for London whether at borough, school or student level. It also helped to identify areas and schools with the most immediate needs, provide appropriate support and monitor improvement.

'Data provided the tool to enable (and at times enforce) a confrontation of the 'brutal facts' about school-to-school standards (both collectively and individually) whilst simultaneously exposing comparisons between schools, and, consequently, the fact that it did not to have to be this way. In this sense it provided a crucial part of the impetus for change, underpinning and fuelling the driving force of 'moral purpose'.

Regional Challenges – A Collaborative Approach To Improving Education, Centre Forum, RM Publications (2014)

The most crucial innovation was the idea of benchmarking school performance against the performance of other schools with similar characteristics, which Brighouse and Woods had piloted on a much smaller scale in Birmingham. This was taken to a different level in London with the annual publication of 'Families of Schools' data, first published for secondary schools in 2003 and running to seven editions after that. Primary Families of Schools data was also published between 2008 and 2010. In the secondary phase, schools were grouped into 23 families of approximately 20 schools based on an average of three years' prior attainment and context data. Prior attainment was calculated on KS2 point scores for all Year 7 students and context data included the proportion of students entitled to free school meals, the Income Deprivation Affecting Children Index (IDACI) data, the percentage of EAL students and a mobility measure. Within each family page a 'performance map' presented schools' average attainment and improvement over three years.

The published data enabled schools across London, for the first time, to compare their outcomes with other schools with statistically similar pupil intakes as well as drilling down into the performance of different subjects. The open publication of this data acted as a great stimulus for school improvement both within schools and across schools and led to some lively debates and effective knowledge sharing. The big message from the data was that 'deprivation was not destiny' and that it was possible to make a step-change in both raising attainment and closing gaps between groups of students and schools. For London's Keys to Success schools in particular, which had been selected on the basis of data, the numbers provided a powerful challenge and stimulus for improvement mediated by London Challenge Advisers. Schools leaders could see at a glance how similar schools were performing and some were forced to confront some uncomfortable messages.

On the other hand, the data showed them where to find the best practice and learn from this. Some Keys to Success schools were 'buck trenders' in particular aspects or subjects and therefore hosted visits themselves, which gave a boost to their confidence and self-esteem. However, it should also be pointed out that the data also provided an improvement stimulus for these schools deemed to be 'coasting' (the *Gaining Ground* programme) and good and outstanding schools where it was demonstrated that compared to similar schools they were under-performing.

The Families of Schools books for both secondary and primary schools were used to:

- Provide a comparative overview of the school's performance for senior school leaders, governors, local authorities and central government.

- Aid self-review and school improvement planning within schools.

- Encourage collaborative activity between similar schools.

- Develop curriculum networks.

- Provide a professional development network of supported professional dialogue.

There were three fundamental questions for all schools to answer:

- How do we compare to similar schools?

- What can we learn from similar schools?

- How can we share knowledge more effectively?

The CfBT's Report on *Lessons From London Schools: Improving Success (2014)*, highlights that the use of data was an almost constant refrain from their interviewees and that 'across the board they identified the potency of well-used data in school transformation in London'. In particular it was the data around groups of underperforming students that made it possible to translate 'moral purpose' into action. The interviewees from those who had played a leading part in the London Challenge stressed the benefits of the project's approach to data as a critical factor in school transformation in London. This had enabled London schools to get ahead of the game in using data forensically in terms of pupil tracking, closing gaps among groups of pupils and between schools and understanding the subtleties of school improvement. The report referred to focus groups of teachers who had lived through the transformation of their schools, where data now dominated their working lives and 'the importance of professional reflection on the patterns found in the data and the power of both internal school comparisons and external school comparisons'.

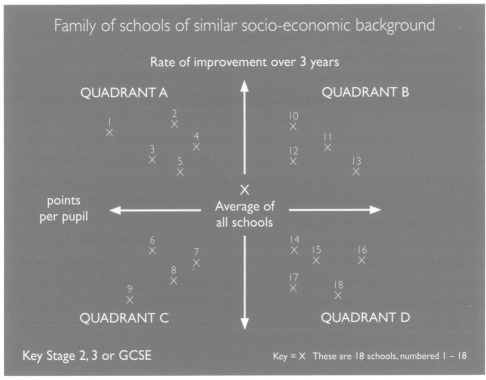

Family of schools of similar socio-economic background

Rate of improvement over 3 years

QUADRANT A

QUADRANT B

1 ×
2 ×
4 ×
3 ×
5 ×
10 ×
11 ×
12 ×
13 ×

× Average of all schools

points per pupil

6 ×
7 ×
8 ×
9 ×
14 × 15 × 16 ×
17 ×
18 ×

QUADRANT C

QUADRANT D

Key Stage 2, 3 or GCSE

Key = X These are 18 schools, numbered 1 – 18

Source: The A-Z of School Improvement: Principles and Practice, Bloomsbury (2013).

Of course, the London Challenge also analysed and used data, including the Families of Schools, in terms of accountability but also as a means of providing high-quality support where it was required. This was particularly true of the Keys to Success schools and helping them drive up standards. Where the data spotlight highlighted that these schools were continuing to perform poorly against similar schools, this often resulted in the creation of new academies to replace them alongside Trusts and Federations. There is little doubt that the forensic use of data was embedded in London's schools from the time of the Challenge, years before national data sets began to publish similar information. The extension of the City Challenge to Greater Manchester and the Black Country saw the same emphases on data and Families of Schools. The lessons learned were incorporated into *The Schools White Paper Of December, 2010 – The Importance Of Teaching*.

Here there was a commitment to publish regional Families of Schools for every part of the country to help schools identify similar schools that were performing differently and from whom they could learn. This took some time to implement and in the end, by 2013, the DfE had produced data on 'similar schools' across the country rather than regionally, but there is some doubt as to whether schools are using this information effectively.

Although the London Challenge came to an end in April 2011 and Families of Schools data is no longer produced for London, the legacy of the Challenge lives on in the real and deep expertise on the use of data embedded in London's schools. There is a shared understanding on how data can be used as a powerful lever for school improvement and a determination to make this happen. This is one of the reasons that Free School Meals and EAL students do so much better in London than elsewhere, as well as London having the smallest gaps in the attainment of different groups of students and being the highest performing region in terms of overall standards.

Further to this, the Challenge made it the norm that performance data should be used systematically in performance management, built around the principles of high professional accountability and transparency at every level in the school. Much earlier than the rest of the country, this led among London's schools to a sustained culture of high expectations and high accountability with targeted support and challenge.

The academies programme

The Labour government's sponsored academies programme ran from 2003-2010 – exactly the period of the London Challenge. The existence of an alternative form of school and governance meant that there was another option when considering what to do with Keys to Success schools, in particular boroughs that were not responding to Challenge and Support.

We have already referred to the five key boroughs where the Challenge and the DfES invested in new academies. The rate of academisation did vary dramatically across London boroughs and where the local authority was performing well such as Camden and Tower Hamlets, there were no academies established in this period. Although there is some debate about the performance of these new academies, the National Audit office studies in 2007 and 2010 reported that, overall, the performance of these academies was impressive with rates of improvement that were better than their predecessor schools.

Whatever else, these new academies with their sponsors acted as a backstop and injected a new sense of purpose and drive into school improvement. Other forms of governance were also tried through the brokerage of the London Challenge such as Federations of Schools between strong and weak schools or Trust Schools with a range of powerful sponsors.

London schools today

A recent study from the CfBT on *Lessons From London Schools (2014)* provided evidence from school leaders and teachers on how many of the barriers to improvement had been dismantled since the early 2000s.

'The attitude of 'what can you expect from these kinds?' had been replaced by a 'no excuses' culture. Schools were more likely to have a strong professional culture and a commitment to continuous improvement'. Further evidence revealed the existence of a strong sense of collegiality and collective responsibility amongst London schools, with a professional pride in their achievements generating further optimism about what more could be done. The summary from the Ofsted study *'Unseen Children'* related to the characteristics of London schools is worth quoting in full.

- Schools that were self-confident institutions with well-motivated staff.

- Highly effective and purposeful leadership.

- Strong networks linking schools with other schools for purposes of improvement and joint practice development.

- A culture of high expectations and 'no excuses' for underperformance.

- Optimism that challenged the inevitability of the connection between poverty and low education outcomes.

All these characteristics have enabled London schools to achieve better results than the rest of the country and continue to improve at a faster rate. The development of the school improvement capacity of London schools has been particularly impressive. The Ofsted inspection of 2010 revealed that on average in England overall, 49% of schools less than 'good' between 2005 and 2013 were successful in raising their grade to 'good' or 'better' when re-inspected. In London the figure is 64%, a remarkable 15% difference, with a significant group of outstanding schools. As well as dealing with the Keys to Success schools, the London Challenge with The London Leadership Strategy managed to 'grow the top' thereby providing even greater capacity to drive system leadership and school improvement across the capital.

The Language of London Challenge

We continue to be inspired by the London Challenge and continue to use its language to impact our work.

Shared vision and values

A compelling and inclusive moral purpose

Ambition and aspiration

Inspirational leadership at all levels

Exceptionality of practice and provision

Striking impact

Progress at a pace

Building capacity

Creating and managing knowledge

A passion for excellence

Innovative and creative solutions

Keys to success

Success against stretching benchmarks

A relentless focus

Fast on our feet

Support and challenge

Perpetual optimism

Unwavering resolve

Powerful partnerships.

Chapter 3

The London Leader
Susan John

The London Challenge and The London Leadership Strategy

Background and context

In May 2003, when the London Challenge was launched, the climate and culture across many London schools and local authorities was extremely competitive. The concept of collaboration was already established through the Beacon School designation process, the Specialist Schools programme and the Excellence in Cities initiative. Leading Edge partnerships were also established in 2003 but the Challenge provided a unique opportunity for school leaders to thrive and establish themselves as regional system leaders.

The London educational landscape is now increasingly more competitive with the emergence of Free Schools but over the past decade, a cultural shift has taken place and there is an acceptance that collaboration and competition can co-exist and that this unleashes a certain degree of dynamism and energy in the system. Indeed, the 2010 Ofsted report on the London Challenge highlights the effectiveness of the excellent system leadership and pan London networks of schools that developed over this period of time.

Origins of The London Leadership Strategy

The London Challenge, originally focusing on secondary education, evolved over time and from 2008-2011 was extended to the primary sector and re-branded as part of the City Challenge expansion to Greater Manchester and the Black Country. The London Leadership Strategy (LLS) led by school leaders for school leaders, under the auspices of the Challenge and the National College, also evolved over this time.

The London Leadership Strategy can best be described as a pan London network of experienced school leaders who have over time played a critical role in establishing the concept that given the right policy conditions, practitioners can lead system-wide transformation.

In 2003, the original team of three headteachers consisted of George Berwick, Alan Davison and Vanessa Wiseman – but by 2011 there were 74 secondary headteachers working across London as part of the Challenge – providing support for more than 50% of London's secondary schools. Throughout the Challenge period and beyond, a core team of headteachers have been responsible for developing and leading the strategy for school-to-school support and system leadership.

An increasing number of London headteachers, convinced by the rigorous and transparent use of data made a moral commitment to be part of the solution to London's problems.

From 2004, the publication of an annual Families of Schools publication meant that there were 'no hiding places' and school leaders had to confront the brutal facts. The three key objectives of addressing the underperformance in London's schools, narrowing attainment gaps and creating more good and great schools resonated with headteachers who were guided by the principles of equity and excellence for ALL London children.

The inspirational and intellectual leadership of the Challenge by Professor Tim Brighouse, Professor David Woods and Jon Coles, coupled with an ambitious vision for London schools was crucial in securing the engagement of all key stakeholders. This meant that headteachers were not only willing to intervene through school-to-school work, but were also given a mandate to intervene.

The National College played a significant role in providing the early Consultant Leader training for headteachers, which was based on a rigorous coaching model and paved the way for the introduction in 2006 of the National Leader of Education designation. The criterion used for the selection of NLEs was based on LLS's selection criteria for Consultant Leaders. By 2011, 20% of London headteachers across the secondary, primary and special school sectors were accredited Local or National Leaders of Education (LLE or NLE.) The College also provided excellent project management support for the core team of headteachers leading the strategy.

The theoretical model

The approach to knowledge management based on the work of Professor George Berwick (Director of LLS, 2003-2008) continues to underpin the work of LLS. It is based upon the belief that the knowledge of how to improve London schools lies within the system.

The four capitals

The theory of action is as follows:

- Create the moral climate for knowledge sharing between staff and schools (Moral Capital).

- Identify those that have the knowledge of effective school practice and capture it (Knowledge Capital).

- Equip the staff and schools with the social skills to share their knowledge effectively (Social Capital).

- Set up the organisational systems for them to share this knowledge with those who need to learn (Organisational Capital).

The LLS identified schools and individuals who could demonstrate outstanding practice, provide the organisational structure to match and move the knowledge around the system and ensured that LLEs and NLEs had the appropriate social and coaching skills to work alongside colleagues in other schools.

Challenge Advisers, as commissioners of school-to-school support developed a strong working partnership with the headteachers, who brokered bespoke school improvement packages based on an audit of need. The matching process was critical, based on powerful data, local intelligence and the deployment of individuals who had the ability to co-construct knowledge in a different context. The pool of Consultant Leaders and latterly NLE/LLEs met frequently as a team, increasing the momentum towards system improvement that focused on large-scale, sustainable and continuous improvement. The practice of using a collaborative, decision-making process based on evidence was crucial to the success of the LLS. Regular meetings of headteachers engaged in this process fostered very strong relationships based on mutual respect and a degree of humility. This approach resulted in highly effective system-wide knowledge management and in this sense the LLS had a high input as a seedbed of ideas that were picked up by the National Challenge across the country.

School leaders have been able to reconcile their own and their schools' interests with the systems. They have recognised that schools providing support will also improve their own outcomes leading to a double lift in performance. This theory is based on the Upward Convergence Model of School Improvement and the continuing need to 'grow the top' if we are to have a sufficiency of strong schools to provide support for the system.

In summary, The London Leadership Strategy embraced the national agenda of transforming schools through enabling innovation to flourish, moving from private improvisation to engage in planned provision using a collaborative learning model. The rigour and high expectations modelled by the headteachers providing support helped to raise ambitions and created a climate of expectation that school collaboration is an inherently good thing for the system.

The most significant intervention programme that ran from 2003-2008 was the 'Keys to Success' programme and by the end of 2003 six headteachers had been recruited to work alongside four secondary schools. The focus of the school-to-school work was on improving leadership at all levels, thereby improving teaching and learning and raising attainment. The Olevi Teaching and Learning syllabus was being developed at this time at Ravenswood School in Bromley, under the leadership of George Berwick, which was widely adopted.

At the beginning of the Challenge, there were 70 schools out of 407 identified as Keys to Success schools based on below 'floor' examination results or being in an Ofsted category of 'serious weaknesses' or 'special measures'. The core team of headteachers leading the strategy attended the annual Challenge Adviser 'triage' meetings held at the beginning of the autumn term and The London Leadership Strategy was commissioned to work with some of the schools requiring intensive support. An important feature of the resource provided was that it was 'in kind' with the supporting school being reimbursed for release of staff time.

By 2006, there were 27 secondary Consultant Leaders, now designated as NLEs deployed across the capital along with eight Special School colleagues. The support provided was bespoke with a clear link to outcomes and NLEs were held accountable to civil servants and the Challenge Adviser team. By 2008 there was only one school in special measures and the number of outstanding schools was rising rapidly. Some of the early Keys to Success schools are now outstanding, most notably, Lilian Baylis Technology School in Lambeth, led by Gary Phillips – an NLE and Director of The London Leadership Strategy.

It was during this time that the concept of a 'red school' package of support was developed by The London Leadership Strategy and the Challenge Advisers. This largely comprised of headteacher coaching, support for middle leadership through the teaching and learning Immersion programme, the improvement of pedagogy through the Outstanding Teacher Programme (OTP) and the Improving Teaching Programme (ITP). Senior staff involved in delivering the teaching and learning syllabi were trained as facilitators and their work was quality assured by external verifiers thereby securing the rigour of the collaborative learning model. The focus on learning through discussion, live teaching, observation, experimentation and reflection was at the heart of the Olevi Collaborative Learning Model.

Additionally, a team of Advanced Skills Teachers (ASTs) across a range of different subject areas were recruited and deployed in schools requiring intensive support. This approach

Olevi Collaborative Learning Model

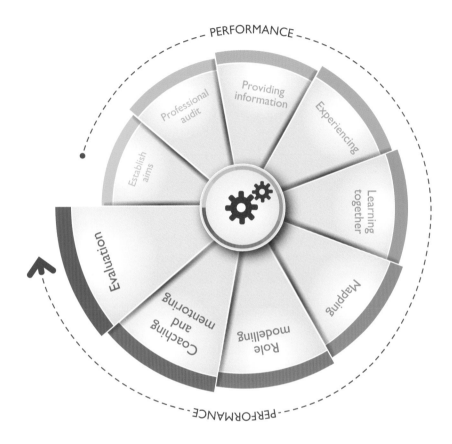

Source: Olevi Collaborative Learning Model

towards school-to-school support was the genesis of the Teaching School model, based on a coaching, triad model of professional development. The 12 secondary schools involved in the London Challenge Teaching School pilot and the 10 primary Facilitation Schools provided their schools as a laboratory for teachers involved in the teaching and learning programmes and de-privatised their pedagogy in a spirit of trust, openness and risk taking.

This work was innovative and based on the concept of trial and error testing in the field. Schools engaged in developing and trialling the model created the discretionary energy required to take such risks and co-created new knowledge for the benefit of the system.

The network of school leaders brokered by the LLS provided much of the expertise to tackle the development needs of schools. The effectiveness of this school-to-school support resulted in sustained improvement over a period of time, through building internal capacity as opposed to a culture of dependency.

As a result of the success of the secondary model, a primary pilot programme was introduced in 2006 and by 2008 a full primary programme was firmly established under the leadership of Robin Bosher, with 70 NLE/LLEs supporting 180 primary schools. The primary programme proved to be both effective and scalable through adopting a triad model of school-to-school support.

At the secondary level there were fewer schools requiring intensive support because they had either improved their performance or had become sponsored academies. This resulted in a situation where the supply of NLE/LLEs was now greater than the schools requiring support and at this point a programme which began as a top-down central school improvement programme developed into a practitioner-led model with a wider vision of school improvement.

In 2007, George Berwick developed the idea of supporting all new secondary London headteachers as part of succession planning and in recognition of the challenges involved in leading complex urban schools. At the same time a 'Good to Great' programme was introduced as part of the strategy to increase the number of Ofsted-rated 'outstanding' secondary schools in London. Politicians, civil servants and the Challenge Advisers supported the diversification of the programme at secondary level.

In a later chapter, Dr Vanessa Ogden highlights the synergy and alignment between politicians, civil servants and the different layers of leadership of London Challenge in her doctoral thesis on the London Challenge, published in 2012.

2008-2011

By 2008, there was a large pool of system leaders in London. Four Pilot Teaching Schools had been established and many others would be designated over the next three years. A tipping point had been reached by year three. The Challenge then entered a mature phase where it had a growing spare capacity with an increasing number of support schools willing to undertake school-to-school work at the same time as the number of schools being directed to accept support was declining.

The leadership of The London Leadership Strategy (LLS) passed to Sue John around this transition phase when London Challenge continued as part of the City Challenge expansion. It was during this period that the trajectory for school improvement to improve the outcomes for all categories of schools developed even further.

Whilst there may have been some initial resistance from schools and local authorities at the beginning of the Challenge, there was now a sense of city-wide pride in the improvements made in London and an increased ambition to create more good and outstanding schools and to narrow attainment gaps.

The project map (see page 58) summarises the breadth of support offered across the capital. Virtually all of the programmes were and continue to be led by serving headteachers who formed a core team, holding each other to account for the progress and success of the programmes.

Gaining Ground

Keys to Success schools continued to receive support and when the 'Gaining Ground' strategy was introduced by the then Department for Children, Schools and Families (DCSF), the LLS was commissioned to broker the London school partnerships. The programme aimed to improve the performance of schools where progress between Key Stage 2 and Key Stage 4 was poor and to increase the number of good schools. Compared to other parts of the country, London was in a unique position to be able to facilitate the sharing of experiences across all the Gaining Ground and Partner schools. Kieran Osborne, headteacher of Hayes School in Bromley, led the programme and not only was feedback positive after the first year, outcomes were improving and schools were committed to working together for the second year of the programme. Funding for this centrally-driven school improvement programme was not continued when the Coalition Government came in to power in 2010. Since then, the newly formed LLS Trust has introduced its own highly successful 'Securing Good' programme, led by Teresa Tunnadine, headteacher of the Compton School in Barnet.

Good to Great

Good to Great (G2G) was conceived by Professor George Berwick and the LLS team, and strongly supported by London Challenge, through Professor David Woods. Andy Buck, the then headteacher of Jo Richardson School in Barking and Dagenham, became the G2G programme lead, working alongside Dame Sue John, LLS Secondary Director and

London Leadership Strategy Project Map

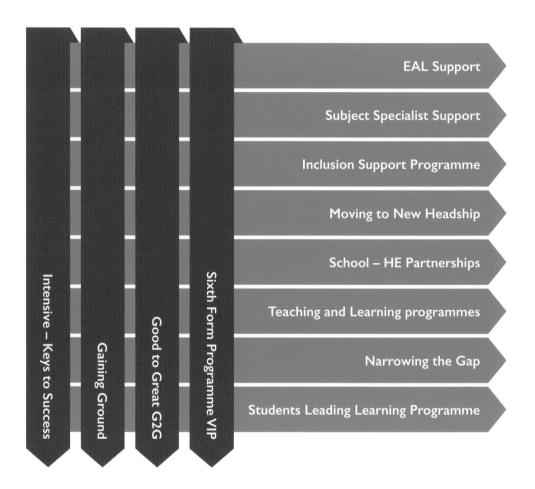

1. All LLS supported schools above the floor A*-C including English and Maths.

2. Proportion of London pupils achieving five or more A*-C grades including English and Maths to continue to be above the national average.

3. Significant improvements in educational outcomes for disadvantaged young children.

4. An increase in the number of outstanding schools in London to 25%.

5. A higher proportion of young Londoners going on to higher education.

headteacher of Lampton School in Hounslow. The programme design was influenced by the Jim Collins 'Good to Great' publication and also relied heavily on input from practising headteachers outlining their own journey towards outstanding.

The aims of the programme were very clear: to have at least 25% of London secondary schools rated as 'outstanding' by 2011 and to have at least two 'outstanding' schools in each local authority and in each London Challenge family. In addition, there was a final aim to improve knowledge sharing, helping to make London's educational system world class.

Schools could elect to become core or associate schools and in return had full access to a programme of support and resources, including conferences, publications, Her Majesty's Inspector (HMI) consultations school planning training, a knowledge sharing network and access to other LLS programmes. Core schools also received a year's support from an NLE.

Peter Matthews conducted an early evaluation of the programme and concluded that some of the key elements that contributed towards its success were based around the ambition and aspiration it generated, the multi-dimensional layers of support and the provision of challenge and support from peer schools.

The programme is an important example of the need for the system to keep 'growing the top' if we are to realise the ambition of creating a self-improving school-led model.

By 2011, 30% of all local authority secondary schools were rated as 'outstanding' compared with a national average of 17.5%. This improvement rate amounted to a 50% increase from the start of the programme and whilst the G2G programme cannot claim to be responsible for all of the increase, a significant number of schools engaged in the programme moved from 'good' to 'outstanding'.

By the end of 2010, leadership of the programme had passed from Andy Buck, who went on to become the Director of Teaching Schools at the National College, to Rachel Macfarlane, who was then Headteacher of Walthamstow School for Girls and who was also leading on the 'Going for Great' programme. The model was also replicated at a subject level with the introduction of G2G conferences for English and Maths subject leaders.

Going for Great

Rachel, who is now Principal of the Isaac Newton Academy, continues to lead this programme, which was designed to support schools that have been judged to be 'outstanding', and helps to maintain their designation and to consider what it is that makes a school great. As already indicated, the programme is still offered as part of the LLS school improvement menu of support and is very popular. The aims of the programme are focused on the capturing and sharing of exceptional practice in the participating schools and supporting these outstanding schools to develop their systemic leadership at a local, national and global level.

There are four seminars each year and they provide a forum for sharing and discussing research and recommended reading, networking and setting up visits to each other's schools and preparing and writing case studies to contribute to an annual publication, which showcases outstanding practice. To date, there have been five publications featuring more than 100 case studies. Successive cohorts of outstanding schools on this programme have produced and refined 'The Nine Pillars of Greatness' – a seminal framework for great schools.

Support programmes for school improvement

In addition to the core programmes, other support programmes for school improvement were developed and delivered separately. The range of support could be matched to the bespoke needs of individual schools and ranged from supporting recently-appointed headteachers to improving sixth form provision, Inclusion support and Subject Specialist support. The LLS core team of headteachers also supported the Challenge by leading and co-ordinating other initiatives, such as the promotion of School and Higher Education partnerships, the DfE, Narrowing the Gap projects and a Student Leading Learning module, training students as classroom observers.

One of the most significant programmes in terms of reach and impact was the Moving to New Headship Programme, which ran as a pilot in 2007 and continued until the end of the Challenge in 2011.

This programme gave an entitlement to coaching to all secondary colleagues starting a new headship, following their appointment through transition to the new post and for the first four terms of headship. The programme was established in response to the Succession Planning agenda of the National College and the increasing numbers of headship vacancies arising across the capital.

Vanessa Wiseman, the then Headteacher of Langdon School in Newham, led and developed the programme. Everyone moving to a new secondary headship in London was offered the opportunity to receive ongoing support from a successful and experienced mentor headteacher. The aim was to strengthen leadership across London schools, to improve the retention of headteachers and to provide a mutually supportive pan London network of newly appointed colleagues.

Over the duration of the programme more than 90 secondary London colleagues took advantage of the support offered and many of the mentor headteachers worked alongside leadership teams, developing policies and providing wise advice in relation to difficult personnel and financial issues. The programme was an excellent example of an 'intergenerational' approach where newly appointed, serving and recently retired headteachers worked together sharing their experience and knowledge. Careful matching of partnerships, based on local intelligence and the challenges different schools faced helped to make this programme so successful, coupled with the ability to be able to partner colleagues across borough boundaries.

One of the other programmes that is worth highlighting in more detail is the Inclusion Support Programme, led by David Bartram, Senior Assistant Headteacher at Lampton School. This programme was introduced in 2009, supported by Paul Harwood, the London Challenge Adviser for Behaviour and Attendance who had identified a link between unsatisfactory behaviour and poor quality Special Educational Needs (SEN) and Inclusion provision.

Newly appointed Special Educational Needs Co-ordinators (SENCOs) and Inclusion managers in many of London schools were keen to receive support from experienced practitioners with a background in Inclusion and SEN. David Bartram put together a team of experienced Inclusion managers and SENCOs who went in to schools initially to audit the provision and then identify areas of strength and developmental needs. A written report for the headteacher would also include a series of recommendations and the continued support of a current practitioner acting as a consultant. By the end of the Challenge, more than 25 schools had received support with Inclusion and participating schools reported improvement in behaviour, reduced exclusions and raised attainment of vulnerable groups of children with special needs.

The Inclusion Support programme is now a central part of the newly formed London Leadership Strategy offer.

In addition to his inclusion support work, David Bartram was responsible for the recruitment, training and deployment of subject specialist Advanced Skills Teachers (ASTs) across the Keys to Success schools. The majority of the ASTs deployed represented the core subjects of English, Maths and Science and the success of their work as middle management system leaders paved the way for the introduction of Specialist Subject Leaders (SLEs).

The nationally accredited Teaching Schools are now responsible for designations and deployment of SLEs.

In 2009, civil servants at the Department for Education were concerned about post-16 achievement in London schools and asked the LLS to develop a programme of support for school sixth forms. Tony Barnes, the then headteacher of Park High School in Harrow developed the VIP programme, focusing particularly on leadership, strategic planning, teaching and learning and accountability practices.

The sixth form programme consisted of a number of component parts, including termly conferences for headteachers and directors of sixth forms, partnership with a consultant headteacher of a successful sixth form and effective use of data through a partnership with London Plus UK. During the final two years of the programme, 50 schools were involved and a VIP leadership handbook was produced. Since 2011, leadership of the programme has passed to Terry Molloy, headteacher of Claremont High School in Brent and Jackie Valin, Headteacher of Southfields School in Wandsworth.

Rob Higgins, formerly Headteacher of Charles Darwin School in Bromley, also worked alongside Professor Malcolm Gillies and Professor David Woods in developing the SHELL programme (School-HE Links in London), which, in addition to the widening participation agenda, also focused on fair access to the more competitive universities.

As can be evidenced by the range of school improvement programmes on offer during this period of time, London was developing its own community of system leaders and this has resulted in a lasting legacy for the post-Challenge period. Steve Munby, the ex-Chief Executive of the National College points to the crucial role played by a cohort of inspired London heads demonstrating effective and sustained leadership through the system. In many respects, this model of system leadership was counter to the executive headteacher role and those involved were passionate advocates of school-to-school work. More importantly, their work contributed to the success of London Challenge. Standards had risen over a seven-year period, the life span of a child attending a secondary school, so that when the Challenge ended, the performance of London secondary schools was more than 4% better than the national average and around 30% of secondary schools were outstanding, compared with only 17% nationally.

It is interesting that Dr Vanessa Ogden cites in her PhD thesis that the London Challenge proved that practitioners can lead system-wide transformation in schools for the benefit of a region's children. Many headteachers involved in the Challenge point to the importance of the refreshing nature of the pan London approach that allowed them to break away from parochial issues and concentrate on what was best for London children.

Regional Challenges are developing across the country and groups of headteachers are seeking to understand the lessons learned from London so that many of the general principles can be applied within their own context. It is fundamental to create moral capital in a region, based on the principles of recognising best practice and a sound track record, alongside collaboration, empathy and above all – trust. To create a regional identity, all groups should be aligned and committed to the development of a collaborative learning model for knowledge transfer and creation. System innovation doesn't just happen – it needs to be planned and regularly reviewed – and school improvement activities must be rigorously and consistently quality-assured.

The key elements of the approach underpinned by our school improvement work in the London Challenge has been recognised in the Centre Forum report on the Regional Challenges, and is summarised as:

"*Relentless and detailed focus on school improvement. Interventions were supported by a theory of school improvement; tailored according to need and circumstances, not a blanket strategy; focused on making schools more outward-looking; supported innovation and growing the top, not just dealing with underperformance; and developed by innovating and investing in what worked. It recognises that school system has the capacity to improve itself provided knowledge could be moved around the system more effectively.*"

London Leadership Strategy post-City Challenge

Was the job finished in London by 2011?

There was a strong feeling amongst all of those involved in the Challenge that whilst the statistics support the view that disadvantaged children have better prospects in London there was still much to be done to continue to improve the life chances of London children. The crucial importance of the London identity that had been created over the period of the Challenge was something that headteachers did not want to lose.

The core team of headteachers responsible for The London Leadership Strategy, led by Dame Sue John, worked closely with Professor David Woods to secure some seed funding from the DfE to support the transition from City Challenge, a central school improvement programme towards a self-improving system. In 2011, Jon Coles, the then Director General at the DfE, allocated a very small pot of money to the secondary and primary LLS teams to support this transition.

There was a huge cultural shift from the City Challenge Programme that had a 'top down' impetus, funded by the DfE with advisers given a remit to challenge and support schools that were targeted for action. Headteachers involved had been identified and appointed to the Leadership Strategies and so it took some time for them to find their place in the new system. The Self-Improving system with its world-class ambitions would focus on bottom-up priorities, funded by money that was considered to be already in the system. Support and challenge was to come from within and leaders would need to be given legitimacy by their peers with schools choosing to participate.

During this period of time (2011-2014), The London Leadership Strategy established itself as a 'not-for-profit' organisation and was registered as a limited company in March 2012. A website showcasing all of the school improvement packages at both secondary, special and primary phase preceded the establishment of the company and was launched in 2011.

The current Chair of The London Leadership Strategy is Professor David Woods and all other directors are either serving headteachers or recently retired headteachers. The directors are responsible for the quality of the school improvement programmes and deployment of NLEs brokered through the organisation, alongside the oversight of the organisation's finances. As the scale of the work undertaken by the LLS has grown, it has become necessary to employ a Managing Director, Anita Kerwin-Nye, and additional project management support.

A range of secondary programmes continue to be offered to schools at every stage of their school improvement journey and whilst the LLS is still London-based, much of the work is also commissioned by other regions, in particular South Gloucestershire, Norfolk and Somerset.

A successful Securing Good programme was developed in 2012, led by Teresa Tunnadine (Headteacher at The Compton School), Jackie Valin (Principal at Southfields Academy) and Mel Adams (Headteacher at St Mary's C of E Primary School) and is now recruiting for its third cohort of schools. In the first year of the programme, 83% of schools that were inspected by Ofsted moved from 'requires improvement' (RI), to 'good' or 'outstanding'. The popular Good to Great and Going for Great programmes continue to be well-attended and the Inclusion support work is expanding.

The LLS has also been successful in securing funding from the GLA to support knowledge mobilisation across the capital and to disseminate the learning from the educational projects funded by the Mayor. Part of this work also focuses on the need to keep London together and maintain the improved educational standards in the capital.

There are now more than 500 schools at primary and secondary level accessing school-to-school support through the LLS. This is an indication that the Ofsted report of 2010 rightly judged that London had developed its own community of system leaders and that this would leave a lasting legacy. It chimes with Steve Munby's description of the London story resting upon the power of purposeful leadership in which London school leaders had a part to play.

GABRIELA MISTRAL

*Mankind owes to children the best
it has to give.*

Their life is fragile.

*If they are to have a tomorrow,
their needs must be met today.*

Many things can wait, but not the children.

*Now is the time their bones are being
formed, their blood composed and their
senses developed.*

We cannot answer them 'tomorrow'

Their name is 'today'.

Chapter 4

The London Teacher
Sara Bubb

The staffing of schools is a fundamental issue. It is often stated that a school's staff is its most important yet most expensive resource – for how can children and young people learn without high quality and committed staff? The McKinsey Report, *How The World's Best Performing School Systems Come Out On Top (2007)*, cites evidence of the cumulative difference that good teaching can make to pupils from early on in their schooling. Between the ages of eight and 11, pupils experiencing high-quality teaching show a 53% better performance than those experiencing low-quality teaching. The effects of high-quality teaching are especially significant for pupils from disadvantaged backgrounds. Research for the Sutton Trust says that for poor pupils, the difference between a good teacher and a bad teacher is a whole year's learning.

Context

At the time of London Challenge, the city had 63,600 (full time equivalent) teachers, a sixth of all the (full time equivalent) teachers in England (434,900). They worked in more than 2,600 schools organised into 33 different local authorities without any overarching body to unite them since the Inner London Education Authority was abolished in 1990.

Teacher recruitment, retention, mobility, experience and quality presented considerable challenges for London state schools. The School Workforce Statistics of 2006 showed that teachers in London had less teaching experience than those in England as a whole: a fifth of inner London teachers had less than three years' and just over one third (37%) had less than six years' service (compared with 15% and 29% of teachers in England). Also, while only 3.8% of teachers in England and Wales were unqualified, in London 10.2% were and in some London boroughs the figure was over 17%. Ofsted found that staff were significantly less likely to be specialists in the subjects they teach in London than is found across the country.

"*Teacher retention and turnover were an issue for many London schools, especially those facing challenging circumstances. Tim Brighouse vividly highlights the effects of teacher turnover when he said: "This can mean that a youngster, during the course of a five-year stay from Year 7 to Year 11 in an average sized challenging school, encountering ten times as many new teachers as more fortunate colleagues in schools further up the pecking order.*"

Bush, 2005: vii

Smithers and Robinson (2005) stated that the extent of teacher shortages in London meant that some schools were *"losing 40% of their teachers every year as more staff take early retirement"*. In one London primary school, the staff turnover was 200%, meaning some teachers did not complete a year.

"It was not uncommon in the most difficult to staff schools for pupils to start the school year with one set of staff members and end it with another. As Brighouse notes, "while some of the senior teachers and those in the management team may stay for a while, the remainder of their teaching staff are often 'here today and gone tomorrow'".

Bush, 2005: vii

London schools had a higher teacher vacancy rate (1.2%): double that of the rest of the country (0.6%). There were higher turnover and wastage rates for teachers in London (23% and 12% respectively) than England (19% and 10%). A significant number moved into the burgeoning independent sector. Around two thirds of the new independent schools in England opened since 2001 were in London.

London's schools made considerable use of Overseas Trained Teachers (OTTs) although the exact number is not known. A survey of OTTs, commissioned by one of the teacher unions, found that most were located in inner city London schools. Three quarters of the headteachers in the sample claimed they had recruited OTTs because no UK teachers were available at the time. The researchers also found that one third had less than four years' teaching experience. Many OTTs are employed by agencies and engaged in supply teaching. Barlin and Hallgarten (2001) estimated that up to 4,000 supply teachers were deployed across London every day in 2000.

These statistics concerning overseas trained and supply teachers, along with the facts that about one in 10 teachers in London were not qualified and that more than one in five pupils were taught by someone with less than three years' teaching experience, presented unique challenges to London's state schools.

How London Challenge Addressed These Issues

The context above concerning the greater use of overseas trained and supply teachers, the number of unqualified teachers, their limited experience and their teaching in non-specialist areas, presents its own set of challenges to London schools.

Pay

The 2003 pay settlement established a new inner London pay scale and provided for a 10% increase in outer London weighting on top of general pay increases. Most importantly, it almost doubled the threshold payment for good, experienced teachers in inner London, providing an incentive for them to stay in (and for others to come to) the capital.

Housing

The cost of housing is a factor in the retention of teachers. Attempts to help teachers afford to live in the capital during the period covered by the London Challenge included the Key Worker Living programme, which was introduced in 2004 and helped almost 5,000 teachers by giving interest-free loans of up to £100,000. The Open Market HomeBuy scheme enabled people to buy 75% of a property, with an equity loan from the government and a lender covering the rest of the cost. The shared ownership schemes allowed teachers to own a minimum 35% share in a property while paying subsidised rent on the rest.

Workplace, well-being and morale

The workplace and staff well-being and morale are vital to retention. Cockburn and Haydn (2004) remind us of the 'soft' factors which can be influential in retaining people: 'friendly colleagues', 'pleasant surroundings', 'intellectual challenge', 'freedom', 'scope for creativity' and 'room for initiative'. A series of surveys of London teachers commissioned by the London Challenge suggest that teachers grew more positive about their work and their workplace: in 2003 less than half of the teachers reported that teacher morale was high. Factors influencing the choice of London school in which to work were varied, but included good working conditions, travel to work distance and being in a location that enables teachers to meet family responsibilities. Factors that may be important but are rarely noted include the cost and stress of travelling to and from school and the availability of parking.

Working in challenging schools is very demanding and requires stamina and resilience. The VITAE report found that teachers in challenging schools were more likely to experience greater challenges to their health, well-being and thus resilience, than those who work in relatively more advantaged schools. While commitment levels did not differ, the consequences for personal health did: in more disadvantaged secondary schools, 63% of teachers reported ill health, compared to 42% in more advantaged areas.

The Institute of Public Policy Research (IPPR) report (2005) for the then DfES – a small scale qualitative study of teachers working in challenging schools in and outside of London –

refers to 'push and pull' factors with regard to what motivates teachers to work in particular schools and these are summarised below:

- Good leadership and a strong, supportive senior leadership.

- Support for learning and development, teaching assistants (TAs), learning mentors, etc.

- Effective systems for dealing with poor behaviour.

- Support at the school level for teachers to learn how to deal with difficult behaviour.

- Good atmosphere and supportive colleagues.

- Opportunities for professional dialogue.

- Team working and good departments.

- Good working conditions, the physical state of the school and resources (staff and equipment).

- Additional classroom support.

- Class size.

- Opportunities for professional development.

Harnessing the best teachers and the best practice

Another group of London teachers which grew during the London Challenge were Advanced Skills Teachers (ASTs). Launched in 1998 (and closed in 2013), the Advanced Skills Teacher grade was a new category of practitioner. All ASTs were assessed and judged to have met a set of standards that describe an excellent classroom teacher. They spent four days a week working in their own school and one day a week in other schools (outreach) to improve the practice of other teachers. There were 640 in post in London – 350 in secondary, 250 in primary and 40 in special schools – representing a sixth of the national total of ASTs.

Whilst this was a national initiative, London made better use of ASTs to improve teaching and learning. Some became London Commissioner's Teachers who were deployed in groups to work in London's most challenging schools.

Chartered London Teacher Standards

Pedagogy and pupil learning

1. Create and manage a classroom environment to ensure a secure and supportive achievement culture and behaviour strategy to meet the needs of London's diverse and mobile pupil population.

2. Apply a wide range of teaching and learning strategies to reduce individual barriers to learning and to meet the variety of pupil needs in London.

3. Develop and implement inclusive practices in a range of learning settings appropriate to the diversity of pupils in London and the complexity of their personal learning, including support for Special Education Needs, to raise pupils' achievements.

4. Progress partnerships within and beyond the classroom with support staff, teachers, other professionals, agencies and community resources, to promote pupils' achievements, learning, development and well-being.

5. Analyse and use relevant data to inform and promote the highest possible aspirations for pupils and to target expectations and actions to raise pupil achievements.

Subject, specialism and/or phase knowledge

6. Demonstrate ongoing development and application of subject, specialism and/or phase knowledge and expertise, drawing on opportunities and resources in London to enrich the learning experience.

7. Identify and use the knowledge and experiences that pupils, their families and other communities bring from outside the school to enrich curriculum development and teaching practices.

Whole school issues

8. Contribute to the development and application of whole school policies and activities to extend opportunities for pupil and school achievements in London.

9. Promote and apply shared professional learning and other forms of support and development for teachers to learn and work together, taking account of teacher mobility, to strengthen collective knowledge and expertise across teachers in London.

Diversity, communities and cultures

10. Build on, extend and apply knowledge of the range of communities, cultures and sub-cultures in London to inform and promote individual pupils' learning.

11. Promote and implement policies and practices that encourage mutual tolerance and respect for diversity, challenge discrimination and widen pupils' understanding of their contribution to society.

12. Demonstrate a capacity to deal constructively and sensitively with conflicting community and cultural values in classrooms and schools.

Teach First also made an impact. It was set up in 2002 for London secondary schools. Teach First allows good graduates to work in challenging London schools for two years. It is specifically designed to attract people who would not otherwise have become teachers and there is a strong focus on recruiting teachers in shortage subjects. Teach First teachers experience a short training course, the Summer Institute, after which they are allocated placements to teach in challenging schools, where they teach a timetable equivalent to that of a newly qualified teacher (NQT). In part, Teach First had been a response to filling vacancies, especially in shortage subjects. The vacancy rates dropped from 3.5% in 2001 to just 1% in 2007. The scheme has been positively evaluated for its impact on London schools through raising expectations and driving change and enthusiasm through young leaders.

The London Challenge set up school-to-school support for professional development and improvement. Many became involved in two long-term professional development programmes: the Outstanding Teacher Programme (OTP) and the Improving Teacher Programme (ITP), which were run by ASTs and local leaders in Teaching Schools such as Ravens Wood. Groups of three teachers per school would undertake the programme, which involved the systematic review of different aspects of teaching and learning, coaching, opportunities to observe outstanding teaching, observation and change management. Key factors in their success were:

- Opportunities to observe outstanding teaching and share practice.

- Coaching taking place in the teacher's own school with the pupils they regularly taught.

- Time for reflection.

- The expertise, communication skills and attitudes of those facilitating courses or providing coaching.

Chartered London Teacher status

Chartered London Teacher (CLT) status was a unique scheme, which the London Challenge set up in September 2004 to recognise and reward teachers' achievements and provide a framework for professional development.

As well as having the prestige of being a Chartered London Teacher for life, when people obtain the award they get a one-off payment of £1,000 from the school budget and Fellowship of the College of Teachers, the body that manages the registration and award process.

Achieving CLT status takes at least two years after registration. People have to have taught in London for at least four years and be on the upper, advanced skills teacher or leadership pay scales by the time they get the award. They have to show how their knowledge, skills and expertise have a positive impact on teaching and learning across the 12 CLT standards and complete a Professional Reflection.

Impact

The scheme captured the interest of many. 'Chartered London Teacher' (CLT) emphasised what schools and teachers had in common rather than what set them apart. The numbers registered rose from 5,000 in July 2005 to 10,000 in February 2006, to 38,000 six weeks later at the end of March 2006. In total, 43,690 registered for the scheme – more than two thirds of all London teachers. Some boroughs embraced CLT more than others. Four out of every five teachers registered in Bromley, Harrow, Richmond and Kingston, but in Westminster and Waltham Forest the proportion was only one in three.

By September 2014, 8,109 people had been awarded CLT status, leaving 35,581 who have registered but not yet completed. Registration for the scheme closed on 1 September 2014 and teachers have until 1 September 2016 to submit an application for CLT status.

The unique feature of CLT was its potential to unify the profession in that it is for all sorts of London's teachers: newly qualified and experienced teachers were working to achieve the same standards. It was also a way of building a coherent approach to an individual teacher's professional development and integrating it with a school's process of professional review and performance management. It was a way to link career and professional development to professional review and school improvement.

In many London schools, all the teachers were registered so the CLT standards and structure became fundamental to professional development, collaboration and aided the development of professional learning communities. CLT status not only offered opportunities for individual teachers but also schools, clusters of schools and local authorities so it was the umbrella that brought organisations and networks together to create a shared picture of effective professional development. The London Challenge set up a wide range of physical and virtual networks:

- CLT e-community.

- Local authority CPD Advisers.

- Primary and Secondary Training School networks.

- A CPD Partnership of strategic organisations such as the General Teaching Council, Training and Development Agency, Specialist Schools and Academies Trust and the National Strategies.

- London Science Challenge and London Maths Challenge.

- Leading London's Learning, a pan London CPD Leaders group.

- London Gifted and Talented networks.

- AST network.

The Pan London EAL (English as an Additional Language) Strategy funded local authorities that had effective teams to support EAL to spread their expertise across London. Hutchings et al (2012) found that this had overwhelmingly positive feedback. This infrastructure was built so that the many pieces of the CPD jigsaw became more joined up and that, by working together, each could achieve more than the sum of the parts.

The scheme contributed to changing the culture of teaching in London and raised the bar of professionalism. Working towards CLT status helped teachers to be more effective in two ways. Firstly, the CLT standards required teachers to be highly effective in key areas that link to the London Challenge's priorities, such as cultural diversity, personalised learning, student voice, improving behaviour and raising standards. Secondly, it formed a substantial pool of teachers with the status to support the development of others and so reduced variation in the quality of teaching and learning within and between schools in London.

The chance to achieve CLT status encouraged teachers to start their career in London state schools and was an incentive for the one in 10 teachers in London who were not qualified to gain qualified teacher status, and so improved the quality of teaching in shortage subjects. The opportunity of CLT status will be an incentive to stay in London state schools because achieving it takes from two to about six years and carries with it a one-off payment of £1,000.

CLT was both a conduit and driver for knowledge transfer, particularly around the standards relating to diversity, communities and cultures. London teachers had more incentive to work together on projects that impact on standards: learning from each other through observation and coaching as well as evaluating the impact of professional development. Because teachers worked towards CLT as part of their day-to-day work and through their schools' performance management and professional development arrangements, all were strengthened.

In conclusion, London schools need a high-quality workforce. The London Challenge was a driver for improvement. It met the criteria proposed by Michael Fullan (2011). It fostered the intrinsic motivation of staff and pupils. It engaged educators and students in continuous improvement of teaching and learning. It inspired collaborative work – and it affected everybody.

What they
have said about
London Challenge

"*The Leaders of London Challenge have motivated London teachers to think beyond their intrinsic sense of duty to serve pupils well within their own school and to extend that commitment to serving all London's pupils well. This has encouraged successful collaboration between London school leaders and teachers across schools. This is a key driver for improvement.*"
Ofsted Report, 2010

"*It shows that schools can be turned around: London's school system, once a renowned catastrophe, is now excellent. It now comfortably beats its hinterland — there is, quite simply, no better place in England for a poor child to get an education.*"
Chris Cook, Financial Times (2012)

"*Most of all we see that it is possible over the period of a decade to take a system with rock-bottom morale and transform into a system of proud achievement with a commitment to continuous improvement. It required tremendous effort to become successful, but the effort was spread over many, who worked together or in concert.*"
Big-City School Reforms: Lessons from New York, Toronto, and London (2014)

"*Perhaps the most effective aspect of the London and City Challenge was that is recognised that individuals and school communities tend to thrive when they feel trusted, supported and encouraged. The ethos of the programme, in which successes were celebrated and the recognition that if teachers are to inspire pupils they themselves need to be motivated and inspired, was a key factor in its success.*"

Merryn Hutchings et al, DfE Evaluation of the City Challenge (2011) London Metropolitan University

---

"*What is clear from our case studies (particularly The London Challenge) is that learning and improvement does not just happen – the best implementation develops strong and consistent mechanisms to get a clear view of what is happening and to inform decisions about what needs to change.*"

Doing Them Justice, London Challenge Case Study Institute of Government, 2014

"*We employed people (for the London Challenge) who we thought 'these are really great people and we really trust them'. So if you've got really great people who you really trust, then you have to back their judgement.......There is something about the ethos about backing the people who you've got doing the job. Make sure you've got great people and back them up.*"

Jon Coles, DfES Director of the London Challenge

"*Established in 2003 to tackle a perceived crisis, the London Challenge set itself an ambitious goal: to completely transform the educational prospects of the capital. The fact that, in little more than a decade, this has come about – and in some style – has ensured that few other education initiatives are so widely (and warmly) discussed… As recognition of the revolution in outcomes in the capital has gradually dawned, the importance of the London Challenge as a collaborative area-based approach to improving education has come to the fore.*"

Regional Challenges – A Collaborative Approach To Improving Education Centre Forum, 2014

"*The quality of education in London and the outcomes for its pupils have been transformed in recent years. The 'London premium' appears to be of greatest value for pupils from low income and ethnic minority backgrounds… nevertheless, pupils do better on average in London than elsewhere in the country regardless of minority ethnic status or eligibility for free school meals. One of the key drivers behind the sustained improvement in London schools was the success of the London Challenge programme.*"

Unseen Children: Access And Achievement 20 Years On – Ofsted (2013)

"The notion that a community of schools could be responsible for its own collective development depends in very substantial measure on the pioneering work of the London Challenge."

Lessons From London Schools
CfBT (2014)

"The success of the London Challenge was founded upon a collective spirit combined with a massive sense of urgency. Settling for the status quo was not an option – a tough line was taken, with radical solutions available and, for the most part, with the support of the various local authority Directors of Education."

Lord Andrew Adonis, Minister for London Schools

"Over time, headteachers came to see themselves as 'London headteachers' responsible for the performance of pupils across London and not just within their own schools. They became actively involved in leading the strategy, supported by Challenge Advisers who were there to broker the best support. Successful leaders and schools were encouraged to organise training for others and there were opportunities for schools to work in partnership in order to share effective practice and exchange innovations."

Ofsted Report (2010)

"In 2002, London was the lowest performing region in the country and it is now the highest performing. This is an unprecedented achievement and is a testimony to the contribution of London teachers and school leaders who have worked hard to raise standards. We have collectively achieved much but there is still more to do."

**Dame Sue John, Director of Secondary,
London Leadership Strategy**

"I've been a London teacher all my life. It wasn't a good place to be in the '70s and '80s and '90s; now it's one of the top performing parts of the country through London Challenge."

Sir Michael Wilshaw, Chief Inspector of schools

"The London Challenge and The London Leadership Strategy harvested very effectively the knowledge, talent, energy and creativity of London's school leaders and teachers to work together to make a much bigger difference to the opportunities and life chances of London's children and young people. We all share the passion and purpose to work, at a pace, to transform our education system so that we can truly make London the leading international city for learning and creativity."

**David Woods, Former Chief Advisor, London Schools, Chair,
London Leadership Strategy**

"There were stark differences between the policy texts of 2003, 2008 and 2010. What commenced as a top-down, centrally driven and government-led approach in 2003 evolved into a practitioner-led strategy for system-wide school improvement. By 2010, headteachers and the London Challenge advisors were the driving force in the policy's development, with a high degree of autonomy albeit within a framework of high accountability for standards."

Dr Vanessa Ogden, Headteacher at Mulberry School For Girls, Tower Hamlets

"London Challenge is a lesson in how to turn around poor pupils' lives... A decade ago, parents were fleeing inner London to avoid sending their children to local schools. Today, a poor pupil is more likely to perform better in the capital than anywhere else in the country."

Dr Tristram Hunt MP, Shadow Education Secretary, December 2013

"London Challenge... worked because it gave many London teachers the leadership, authority and support they needed to challenge and learn from each other. It became the mission of every teacher in a London school to improve standards across the city."

Rt Hon Nick Clegg MP, Deputy Prime Minister, October 2013

"The London Challenge injected fresh ideas and optimism into the system. It challenged the lazy notion that disadvantage was inevitably associated with underachievement. Crucially, a major focus for London Challenge was on improving the quality of school leadership."

Steve Munby, CEO of CfBT Education Trust

"London Challenge was a great success. But it was not a single thing: it was a package of policies. It included school-to-school support, it included the development of the Chartered London Teacher scheme, it included improvements to teacher supply; it included academisation of schools. These were not done to a pre-ordained plan: they were customised to different settings. We look back on a policy initiative called London Challenge, but it wasn't like that as it developed…"

Professor Chris Husbands, Director at the Institute Of Education

---

"A recent flurry of academic and thinktank studies have pointed to the significance of the Labour government's initiatives in the 2000s, most notably the London Challenge. The scheme, established in 2003, paired successful headteachers with those in less well-performing schools. In doing so, it nurtured a strong network of professional support, as well as a sense of shared identity and mission. By opening up schools to new influences and encouraging great leaders to mentor others, the London Challenge fostered a spirit of collaboration."

Munira Mirza, London's Deputy Mayor For Education And Culture

"*Don't allow yourself to be isolated.*

Remember there are people out there who share your belief that the world can be a better place and know, like you, that what you do is the bedrock of social justice, political freedom and that there exists a sort of slavery which is mental as well as economic and that, like you, they have pledged themselves to destroy it.

What you do is the most important job in the world and you are doing it where its most needed."

Sir Tim Brighouse, Commissioner of London Schools (2003-2007)
Message to London's School Workforce

"*It is important to continue the momentum that London has established and share it with the rest of England. London Challenge showed us there is a recipe for success. There is no 'magic bullet' and we must continuously learn and adapt to meet children and young people's educational needs. Ongoing London Challenge programmes that run throughout England, as well as research in to what worked, enables us to do this through peer-to-peer support and evidence-based practice.*"

Anita Kerwin-Nye, Managing Director of The London Leadership Strategy

"We are seeing a renaissance in our urban centres and in the schools that are keys to their success. As Minister for London Schools since 2002, I have had the privilege of witnessing at first hand the commitment and success of headteachers, school staff and local authorities across the capital."

Stephen Twigg, Minister for London Schools

"London Challenge has continued to improve outcomes for pupils in London's primary and secondary schools at a faster rate than nationally. London secondary schools continue to perform better than those in the rest of England. Progress or support for schools are planned with experienced and credible London Challenge Advisers using a shared and accurate audit of need. Excellent system leadership and Pan-London networks of schools allow effect partnerships to be established between schools enabling needs to be tackled quickly and progress to be accelerated."

London Challenge Ofsted Report (2010)

Chapter 5

The London Student
David Woods and Tim Brighouse

Before providing a mid-London Challenge snapshot of the socio-economic make-up of London's students, it is worth making a preliminary and important point. We felt we could have less impact on the London Student than was possible with the London school itself, the London Teacher and the London Leader. Apart from the obvious point that we could affect them even more indirectly than the other three identified elements, there is the well recorded point that children between birth and 16 spend more than 80% of their waking time outside school and therefore marginally less than 20% in school. What happens in school, of course, is vital so far as learning is concerned. We can affect that time in school by helping schools improve and by focusing on the vital role of teachers. It is possible too, to help schools learn from each other by involving students more in their learning and in playing a leading and responsible role in school life, although it has to be acknowledged that this is the Cinderella of all the processes of school improvement.

What the London Challenge did not do was try to affect, except at the margins, what happened to students in the home and the community. We had to prioritise and we knew that the London boroughs themselves through their housing policies and practices and, for example, in how they support 'looked after children', would be having different effects on those influences.

We shall describe what we did at the margins after setting out the facts.

In 2007, when the Challenge turned its attention to primary as well as secondary schools, London was home to 1,213,870 pupils under the age of 18 – and 29% of them were eligible for free school meals (40% in inner London) against an average of 15% in England as a whole. 24% of children in London lived with only one parent and 29% lived in overcrowded households. The most distinctive feature of London's children was their diversity. Two fifths of them belonged to a black, African or minority ethnic group and one third spoke English as an Additional Language (EAL) with some 300 languages being spoken overall. This diversity was allied to another distinguishing feature – the high level of inequality in life chances and outcomes.

The Mayor of London's Children Report (2007) states: "*The diversity and inequality, which so clearly characterises London, are even more apparent in relation to London's children. Indeed London's children can be understood to be unique, both in terms of their diversity in relation to children nationally, and in terms of the specific inequalities, challenges and issues which they, their families and their communities face. London's children have themselves highlighted what they see as some of these challenges, including housing, the environment, mobility, racism, bullying and criminality."* It is against this background that the Challenge had to demonstrate that 'deprivation and demographics are not destiny'.

It was estimated that 41% of children lived under the poverty line (51% in inner London) compared with 28% of children in the UK as a whole. London had the highest pupil mobility in the country with large numbers of children joining or changing schools at non-standard times. International migration, housing problems, family break-up and low income were key factors, often interrelated. Many of these children needed additional language or learning support to achieve well. At the beginning of the London Challenge the aspirations of young people and their communities was said to be often too low. Some communities remained insular which restricted young people's horizons and limited their future opportunities. Raising their aspirations was crucial to tapping their potential and improving their achievement at school. Young people had to be encouraged to aim higher and engage more with the opportunities and wealth of resources that London provided and experience the advantages that learning in London could provide. London had the potential to inspire and enthuse. Its rich history, cultural treasures, business, leadership and sporting traditions were and are a natural magnet for people at the leading edge of their career but many young Londoners never experienced this side of their city. Therefore, one of the first ideas of the Challenge was to consult on the details of a 'London Student Pledge' which set out the key experiences that every young Londoner should enjoy during their time of school, awakening them to what their great city had to offer and encouraging them to be more ambitious about their future. Of course, most London schools had always offered a range of activities and experiences but this was an attempt to codify these both in and outside school.

The London Student Pledge

Ten things that every London secondary student should experience:

- To have the opportunity early in their time at secondary school to have their achievements formally recognised, perhaps in assemblies and celebration evenings.

- To take part in a public event such as a sports match, musical performance, public speaking or painting exhibition.

- To be involved in a school play, musical or reading, either as an actor or by helping to produce it.

- To take part in a residential course or visit that will further their education.

- To have the opportunity to help others in a voluntary activity.

- To attend an artistic, sporting or cultural event at one of London's major venues.

- To have opportunities to understand and celebrate diverse cultures and to extend their international knowledge, understanding and experience.

- To engage in an enterprise that requires planning, design, completion and review. Examples could include running a school shop, building a new machine or helping with the design of a new school facility.

- To make use of cutting-edge learning technologies, including online learning to extend their knowledge and understanding.

- To contribute their views on London issues and have their voice heard.

In order to ensure that London secondary schools should have ready access to what in effect is an extraordinary 'commonwealth' of opportunities afforded to children and students in London, the small team of civil servants led by Jon Coles arranged meetings to promote access to museums, art galleries, theatres and music facilities, together with the many other distinctive venues and events which enrich the capital.

Many schools, encouraged by the Challenge, and brokered links to London's 'commonwealth' of cultural treasures, developed their own Pupil Pledge based on this template, considerably extending opportunities. There is a debate about how much London pupils benefit from the economic and cultural dynamism of the city (see Lessons From London Schools, CfBT Education Trust).

'Although large numbers of pupils do live in poverty and experience disadvantage, London is also a place of employment opportunities and higher than average salaries... higher job density than any other region... Could it be as a consequence of this dynamic environment, London's pupils aspire higher than their non-London counterparts?'
Ibid, p52

It can be argued that simply by living in London, young people have access to a range of opportunities and possess a greater drive to succeed. Researchers suggest that the context of local, economic opportunities may feed into educational attainment via its role in shaping

Case Study –
Student Pledge at
The Compton School,
Barnet

I was made aware of the London Challenge Student Pledge by Teresa Tunnadine, my headteacher in 2008, when I had whole school responsibility for student leadership. Our priority for student leadership development was to encourage students to participate more fully in London life to enrich their cultural and historical enjoyment and to develop skills and interests which they would be able to take into adult life. The London Challenge Student Pledge resonated with the London-based enrichment activities we were so keen to encourage our students to get involved in as well as offering a new direction for student leadership that was more relevant, more student-focused and which offered opportunities for further increasing students' social capital.

Firstly, I created a student pledge leadership group of motivated Year 9 students to lead on the design, launch and coordination of a Compton School version of the London Challenge pledge – this was in itself an opportunity for students to demonstrate their ability to lead – but the fact that the programme was peer-led undoubtedly helped to contribute to the uptake of the pledge by students when it was launched. Student pledge leaders came up with ideas based on the London Challenge Student Pledge that would be relevant and enjoyable for our students. They decided to focus on students in Years 7-9 only and students involved had to make a commitment to take part in 15 enrichment activities by the end of Year 9.

There were three levels – bronze, silver and gold – to enable students to progress through a range of activities, which gradually became more challenging with recognition being given as each level was completed. We then coordinated a programme of enrichment activities –some of which were school-based and some of which were based further afield in local and central areas of London – and actively encouraged students to participate in them. Each half term, students would be celebrated in assembly in recognition of the number and range of pledge activities which they had participated in and they would share their experiences with their tutor groups. The student pledge leaders also put a huge amount of energy into the launch of the pledge, creating a video and an electronic recording system, which significantly helped to encourage uptake (this was 2008!). Once the launch had taken place, we continued to identify opportunities such as end of year celebration evenings, transition visits and governing body meetings to help embed the pledge and to highlight the importance of student participation in the life of the school. Furthermore, a number of opportunities for sharing the success of the Compton Student Pledge with other schools arose and student leaders were selected to make presentations, resources and activities that staff and students could adapt to use in their own schools.

Although the Compton Student Pledge has now been superseded by other student leadership and enrichment programmes, it undoubtedly acted as a springboard for so many of our students, staff and parents, to realise the benefits of participating in cultural activities both in and beyond the school (our programme of enrichment activities increased and our participation registers showed an increase in the numbers and groups of students who took part in at least one cultural activity). The student pledge leaders who co-developed the programme found something in the original concept of the London Challenge Student Pledge which inspired them to want to participate in cultural activities and to encourage their peers to do the same. Although these particular students have now left the school, the high profile given to student leadership in the school today is definitely part of their legacy and that of the London Challenge Student Pledge.

Louise Taylor, Associate Headteacher

young people's educational aspirations and expectations and contributing to enhancing pupils' engagement at school. However, while this might be a contributing factor, it does not in itself explain the remarkable rise in pupil attainment during these years.

Improving behaviour and attendance

Other London Challenge programmes for students were concerned with improving behaviour and attendance working in partnership with local authorities and schools. At the beginning of the Challenge, poor pupil behaviour and attendance were significantly greater problems in London than elsewhere and this was a major factor holding back achievement in the Keys to Success schools. Most London local authorities became part of the Behaviour Improvement Programme, a national programme adapted by the Challenge for London. Specific funding was targeted at improving behaviour and attendance and supporting students at risk of exclusion and with serious social problems whilst ensuring that excluded pupils received a full time education.

A specialist London Challenge Adviser acted as a catalyst for change to create leverage for rapid improvement in behaviour and attendance. A very effective audit tool was developed to identify and prioritise issues for action in schools and support was brokered from a wide range of agencies including National Strategy Regional Advisers, expert local authority staff and agencies that offered specialist services in restorative justice, resolving conflict, residential experiences and behaviour management. The impact of all this joint activity was a key feature in transforming many Keys to Success schools in terms of attainment and achievement.

Provision for gifted and talented young people

The London Challenge also took advantage of national policy to develop much more personalised education in schools tailored to the needs of the students to both raise aspirations and engagement. The gifted and talented education arm of the Challenge extended the work already developed in Excellence in Cities schools throughout London, benefiting both primary and secondary pupils.

A consortium, including local authorities and higher education partners, was funded to run the programme with a new London Centre for gifted and talented young people. Programmes were provided virtually as well as at the centre. Professional development centres, equipping teachers to support gifted and talented pupils in the classroom were also supported by online resources. Clusters of local authorities and schools were developed to spread good practice more widely and to involve the wider educational community and the business, sports and cultural sectors. A concerted effort was made to ensure that youngsters from London were strongly represented in national programmes such as the National Endowment for Science, Technology and the Arts and the Centre for Gifted and Talented Youth summer programmes at Warwick University.

Ethnicity

In several of the evaluations of the London Challenge and the success of London schools, a potential explanatory contextual factor concerns the ethnicity of pupils. There are proportionally fewer white people in London than in the rest of England – the Department for Education's figures in 2013 record about 30% in inner London and about 50% in outer London. Ofsted's *Unseen Children: Access And Achievement 20 Years On (2013)* report demonstrated that white British pupils from disadvantaged backgrounds were consistently the lowest performing of all the main ethnic groups and that gaps in attainment to other groups have widened over time. This is undoubtedly true of the national picture but not in London. The CfBT's study *Lessons From London Schools (2014)*, analysing trend data in GCSE performance for different ethnic groups, reveals that '*all ethnic groups have improved their performance considerably and in addition gaps have been closed between them*'.

Between 2004 and 2012, the attainment of black pupils in London rose by 36%, white pupils by 29%, and pupils of mixed ethnicity by 28%. Although Chinese and black pupils still made up the top and bottom of the distribution, the difference in their attainment had narrowed from 37% to 14%. The study argues that the London improvement cannot be attributed to specific ethnic groups and that white pupils constituted one of the significantly improved groups. They go on to say that '*the data suggests that something extraordinary has taken place in London, not just for some ethnic groups but for all ethnic groups... London's success is not a consequence of the difference in cultural values displayed by ethnic groups in the capital*'.

However, London's overall improvement rate has benefited from significant gains made by minority groups concentrated there and there are some theories that building a culture of ambition and aspiration is more achievable in communities where, despite deprivation, education is both highly valued and seen as the great opportunity for economic and social advancement. The example of Tower Hamlets with its dominant Bangladeshi community is often cited as a good example of this but white, disadvantaged students also do well there (see *The Tail*, 2013).

An analysis of the GCSE data between 2003-2011 shows that pupil performance moved from being the lowest region in the country to the highest and that this continued to be

Percentage of 5 A*-C GCSEs including English and Maths

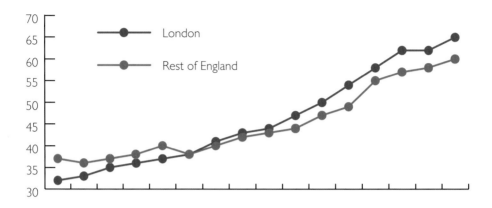

Source: Regional Challenges – A Collaborative Approach To Improving Education,
Centre Forum, RM Publications (2014)

sustained beyond the end of the Challenge, with 64% of pupils achieving five or more GCSEs at grades A*-C including English and Maths, compared to a national average of 59% (2013 data). Inner London pupils also performed above the national average despite considerable socio-economic disadvantage. There has been some discussion as to whether this has been achieved by concentrating resources on 'borderline students' to push them over the grade C threshold at the expense of the educational needs of other students. While that will certainly be true – just as it is in the rest of the country – the *Social Mobility and Child Poverty Commission Report (2013)* calculated the proportion of pupils achieving eight A*-Bs in London and concluded that the performance was higher than other regions for all pupils, including those from disadvantaged groups, and that London's pupils were exceeding expectations whatever the measure.

Similarly, the Centre Forum report on *Regional Challenges (2014)* modelled attainment against the new proposed measures of 'Progress 8' and demonstrated that secondary schools in London made an average of at least half a grade more progress in each subject than in the lowest-performing regions and were the top performing 'progress' region. A simple focus on overall regional headline outcomes underplays the true scale of London's turnaround for its most disadvantaged pupils but it is here that the gap in performance between the capital and elsewhere is most evident. Half of pupils from disadvantaged backgrounds now achieve five A*-C EM, elsewhere it is around one third.

How the regions measure up: modelling the new Progress 8 measure by region using 2013 data

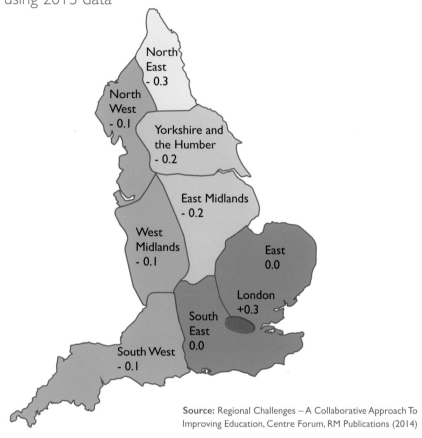

North East
- 0.3

North West
- 0.1

Yorkshire and the Humber
- 0.2

East Midlands
- 0.2

West Midlands
- 0.1

East
0.0

London
+0.3

South East
0.0

South West
- 0.1

Source: Regional Challenges – A Collaborative Approach To Improving Education, Centre Forum, RM Publications (2014)

At primary, fewer than one in five Free School Meals (FSM) pupils are currently failing to reach the basic expected level of literacy at Key Stage 2 whilst in the lowest regions it is one in three. London has the 10 best performing local authorities in this category, in which 85% of all FSM pupils reach the expected literacy levels. The London Challenge programmes paid particular attention to 'closing gaps', especially between 2008-2011, for both phases, working closely with the London boroughs. The result is that between 2004 and 2012, there has been a marked improvement for pupils in the more deprived half of the population and there is now a pattern of greater equity in London schools than elsewhere. If you are a pupil from a deprived background in school in London, you are likely to attain better results than a similar non-London pupil.

Put simply, London is the best place in the country for a disadvantaged child to be educated and the powerful message is that this decoupling of deprivation and destiny appears to have been achieved to a greater extent by many pupils in London's schools. The Centre Forum report – *Regional Challenges (2014)* suggests that the London evidence '*supports the idea that there is a real need to change the narrative around the performance of disadvantaged pupils in other parts of the country*', something also stressed by Ofsted's *Unseen Children Report* in 2013.

At its simplest level, the staffroom despairing rhetorical comment: 'What more can you expect from children from backgrounds like this?' which was so prevalent in earlier decades, seems to have been almost eradicated from London school staffrooms. We would claim that if this is the case, it would be unsurprising since it was the message conveyed by Brighouse as the first Chief Adviser as the difference between his time in London schools 27 years earlier and his time in them during the Challenge. As we all suspect, teacher expectation coupled with their skill and a response from the student can change student outcomes.

The transformation in pupil outcomes in London is an educational phenomenon with profound implications for driving social mobility. The London Challenge succeeded in changing the narrative and mindset so that London's schools and their pupils could meet the highest of expectations.

"_Give them teaching that is determined, energetic and engaging. Hold them to high standards. Expose them to as much as you can, most especially the arts. Root the school in the community and take advantage of the culture the children bring with them. Pay attention to their social and ethical development. Recognise the reality of race, poverty and other social barriers but make children understand that barriers don't have to limit their lives… Above all, no matter where in the social structure children are coming from, act as if their possibilities are boundless._**"**

Charles Payne

Chapter 6

London Challenge And Partnership Working
David Woods And Tim Brighouse

The London Challenge (2003)

Partnerships and alliances were essential for the London Challenge for a number of reasons. It was never going to be a top-down micro-managed set of policies and practices, rather more an attempt to influence by persuasion various participants in a loosely coupled system. As the prospectus set out, it was necessary to enlist the help and expertise of many if it was to have optimum effect.

So far as schools, clearly the principal agents of change and progress, were concerned, we have written elsewhere about schools working in partnership with each other through the work of The London Leadership Strategy. Excellence in schools was cultivated through collaboration with others and then spread for the benefit of all.

But there were other alliances too. It was the task of the small group of civil servants led by Jon Coles, to act as expediters of these alliances enlisting the presence and support of key players and chasing progress by partners and allies committed to supporting the Challenge programme and its various participants.

For each alliance or partnership to be successful in any situation, there are various conditions that need to be met.

Do the partners have shared understanding and sympathy with the overall purpose, in this instance a transformation in the outcomes for students of London schools? Clearly even the many people in London who work there but live in the commuter belt beyond Greater London have a vested interest in the health of the capital's future. And so it proved to be. People in the City, in universities, in the world of the arts and many of those running prestigious private schools in the independent sector were only too ready to give their time and other resources to add value to the Challenge.

Secondly, are there shared values among those participating? In the case of the schools, there was a high degree of alignment in values. In the other looser alliances, there was probably less congruence, although it was accordingly less important.

Thirdly, is there clarity of 'who does what' within the various alliances described on upcoming pages? This is usually the weakest point within alliances but within the London Challenge Jon Coles and his team were tireless in ensuring it didn't flounder for want of clarity or people knowing what they were committed to seeing through. A vivid example of that is the way in which London boroughs became involved in solving panLondon issues.

Fourth and finally, are there agreed 'success criteria' for the collective outcome of the alliance and are there dates when reviews would take place? Again, apart from the private accounting to Number 10 which Jon Coles largely dealt with, the overall scheme was twice reviewed by Ofsted.

The shared ambition of the London Challenge to transform standards therefore was also fostered by a range of other partners – local authorities, higher education institutions, business and education and social agencies. In all this a sense of identity was important, underpinning the need for the London-wide solution which overrode other jurisdictions, governance structures and boundaries.

Partnerships with local authorities

Effective partnerships with London's 33 local education authorities were vital to the success of the London Challenge. Because of their small size, some of these authorities were fragile and lacking robust and consistent support for their schools at the time of the introduction of the Challenge. Some inner London areas faced very great challenges in improving results. The decision was taken in 2003 to focus on five key boroughs in particular that were seriously underperforming and required the greatest support – Hackney, Haringey, Islington, Southwark and Lambeth. Action plans were developed with these five boroughs in particular to provide significant investment in new academies, establishing new schools through competitions and increasing sixth form provision. In some of these boroughs, new organisations were already in place such as the Hackney Learning Trust and Cambridge Education (CEA) Islington which helped drive the pace of change in co-operation with the Challenge. In others, there had to be greater 'political' challenge to ensure radical change.

All London's local authorities were able to benefit from London Challenge programmes to improve leadership, teaching and learning and to raise standards and close gaps. Every local authority over the period of the Challenge had designated secondary or primary, or both, Keys to Success schools with their own dedicated London Challenge Advisers and central resources. Challenge Advisers were allocated to every local authority working alongside their school improvement teams in a focused way to support local efforts to change the culture and expectations to produce a visible transformation not only of the infrastructure, but also in what people believed could be achieved. Of course in this period there were always high performing authorities such as Westminster, Kensington and Chelsea, Camden and Tower Hamlet, and part of the objectives of the Local Authority Reference Group established by Tim Brighouse, the first Commissioner of London's schools and previously a highly successful Director of Education in Birmingham, was to share best practice and common issues.

In the later years of the Challenge, local authorities were encouraged to work together in clusters on school improvement issues. Although there was some resentment in the beginning that the London Challenge was 'taking over' the school improvement function of the local authorities, good partnership working and active collaboration between the Department for Education and Skills (DfES) civil servants, London Challenge Advisers and the local authority's Head of School Improvement and their teams, meant that there was a climate of mutual support and challenge which benefited the schools and their students as can be seen from the significant gains in outcomes. By 2008, all of the original 'key boroughs' had experienced dramatic gains in overall attainment and in closing attainment gaps, so much so that the attention for the last three years of the Challenge switched to other boroughs that they had overtaken such as Greenwich and Croydon. Throughout this period and beyond, almost all London's local authorities were quick to take advantage of a range of Challenge initiatives and through 'collaborative competition' to drive up standards. Working with the London Challenge in partnership the leadership of local school improvement services improved significantly.

There was a tougher approach to the performance of heads and schools, a much stronger emphasis on the use of data and on providing effective professional development. If there was a sticking point in the relationship between central government and local government, it was sometimes around the decision to close or 'fresh start' schools as academies free from local education authority control, which brought other providers into the system. Although Challenge Advisers worked in partnership to improve Keys to Success schools and invested in them, if there was little or no progress after two years or so, there had to be a debate over the best way to make progress which would often result in a structural solution.

Overall, however, partnerships between the London Challenge and the local authorities remained positive and productive and the continuing success of London schools is testimony to the effectiveness of this work. The Challenge acted as a catalyst to improve collective education provision robustly tackling underperformance and progressively improving standards so that by 2009, London had been transformed from the lowest-performing region in the country to the best performing.

Partnerships with higher education institutions

Improving progression to higher education was always an ambition of the London Challenge and London has one of the world's largest concentrations of higher education institutions (44). In 2005-2006, some 24% of the cohort of 18 year-olds in London were engaged in higher education, but as well as increasing this percentage, the Challenge aimed to increase participation from low participation neighbourhoods and lower socio-economic classes. To do this, the Challenge worked in partnership with higher education institutions helping them work more closely with the local schools and further education colleges.

Some secondary schools already had very good links with universities, but the ambition was that every secondary school in London (over 400 schools) should have an identifiable, main university link and that a higher proportion of young Londoners would go on to higher education including the more competitive universities. Working with Aim Higher, London Higher, the Higher Education Funding Council and London's schools, colleges and universities, quality partnerships were developed and fostered. Professor Malcolm Gillies, a Higher Education Champion for London was appointed from the group of University Vice Chancellors to encourage the vision of partnership working to become a reality. He jointly chaired the SHELL (School-Higher Education Links in London) programme with Professor David Woods.

Partnerships were to be based around one or more priorities from a menu of options including:

- Information, advice and guidance supporting progression in higher education.

- Mentoring and coaching relationships for students in London schools.

- Investment in the development of academies and trust schools.

- Engaging in institutional governance arrangements.

- Gifted and talented education, including outreach and other support.

- Professional and curriculum development.

- Provision of higher education-level study in schools and colleges and delivery of diplomas.

To support the aspirations for enhanced participation in higher education, it was essential to ensure that gifted and talented pupils from disadvantaged backgrounds were encouraged to aim higher and achieve their ambitions. From September 2008, 1000 London students in Year 10 who were eligible for Free School Meals (FSM) were to be identified to undertake a four-year support programme to secure a place on a course at their target university. In return for continual progress against challenging targets, these students received an entitlement of £400 a year to spend on relevant external activities. The vision was that every London school and further education college would be able to access co-ordinated outreach and support for their gifted and talented learners from higher education institutions throughout their region and beyond. Other key partners such as businesses and independent schools were linked to this network. All this had a very positive impact – young people in London are more likely to progress to higher education than any other region in the country and the most recent government data (2013) indicates a dramatic gap: a higher education participation rate of 43% against the national average of 35%.

Partnerships with governors and parents

It has to be said that there was no strategic or systematic attempt to involve governors directly in the London Challenge programme overall apart from particular school improvement programmes. In the Keys to Success programme, governors participated in School Improvement Boards made up of the London Challenge Adviser, Senior School Leaders, governors and local authority representatives. The purpose of these boards was to monitor and evaluate the school's action plan for improvement including the use of resources and the need to broker and commission extra support. This was usually done on a half-termly basis and formed an important 'engine' for improvement with reports back to full governing bodies. This gave governors some ownership of the improvement plan along with the accountability and proved a very useful mechanism for 'getting the best out of everybody' in the interests of the school and its students.

There were, however, occasions when this failed to work and the school did not improve, leading to central government, through London Challenge Officers, deciding to seek radical solutions. The Gaining Ground Programme, a national programme adapted in London, is another example of when governors were involved in charting further improvement. In a general sense, governors were kept well informed about the aims, objectives and progress of the Challenge and apart from those directly involved with schools needing to improve, other governors of good and outstanding schools were asked to support their headteachers and sometimes other staff in supporting other schools which they generally did realising that there were benefits for their own school too.

With regard to parents, there were several initiatives to keep them well informed about the London Challenge, especially if they were involved with Keys to Success schools. Parents as well as students and teachers were regularly invited to events and celebrations. From 2003-2007, there were annual surveys of parents to measure parental satisfaction with the progress of London's schools and there were similar annual surveys for pupils. The results of these were used to fine tune existing programmes of improvement and to commission others.

Other partners and providers

It was important that everybody played their part in meeting the London Challenge – businesses, media, sporting and cultural spheres, special providers of services – all had their part to play. The London Challenge was born out of the perception by politicians that there were far too many schools that were failing to inspire and lead their communities and far too many areas where education aspirations were too low. The Challenge was to harness the creativity and dynamism of a great world city so that a range of agencies and organisations could get a business challenge which was investigated in 2003 to encourage employers and city firms to get behind the efforts of London schools and ensure that every school was backed by support from a business to raise standards and improve the life chances of their students.

Businesses also came forward to sponsor education events and initiatives and to celebrate successes. A dramatic example was the annual flood lighting of the Shell building on the riverside illuminating, in more senses than one, the continuing success of London schools. Another was the donation of many poster sites to celebrate the successes of London's students. Prestigious centres in London such as the Science Museum, the Tate Gallery, the Transport Museum and various universities were made available to celebrate the work of schools, teachers and students. As the London Challenge matured, marketing campaigns from 2008 produced t-shirts, mugs, Oyster-card holders and tube maps to solidify the aim of instilling pride and a common identity amongst London's schools, teachers and students.

The Challenge had a relatively small team of civil servants, advisers and headteachers to develop and deliver programmes. It was essential to build capacity by engaging a range of other providers. A key provider was Education London, an agency that employed expert practitioners in other subjects and school improvements that could be commissioned by London Challenge Advisers to work in depth in London's most challenging schools. The Challenge was also able to draw upon the best practice of the National Strategies and their regional advisers to support particular schools. Promoting good behaviour and attendance was an essential element of London Challenge support and the Challenge

Adviser for this aspect of work was able to draw upon a range of providers, trusts and charities who could provide expert guidance and training on dealing with bullying and poor behaviour, pupil support systems, poor mentoring, restorative justice programmes and improving attendance.

Similarly, in a city where 300 languages are spoken and almost 50% of students in inner London are English as an Additional Language (EAL) learners, it was vital to broker and commission support for EAL provision. This was mainly drawn from the best of local authority and school practice leading to the formation of the Pan London EAL Strategy with a Register of EAL expert consultants.

The London Challenge was able to bring together many partners in a common cause linked to a powerful, shared narrative of raising aspirations so that education provision and performance could be transformed in the capital city.

SEAMUS HEANEY –
THE CURE AT TROY

History says, don't hope

On this side of the grave.

But then, once in a lifetime

The longed-for tidal wave

Of justice can rise up,

And hope and history rhyme.

So hope for a great sea-change

On the far side of revenge.

Believe that further shore

Is reachable from here.

Believe in miracles

And cures and healing wells.

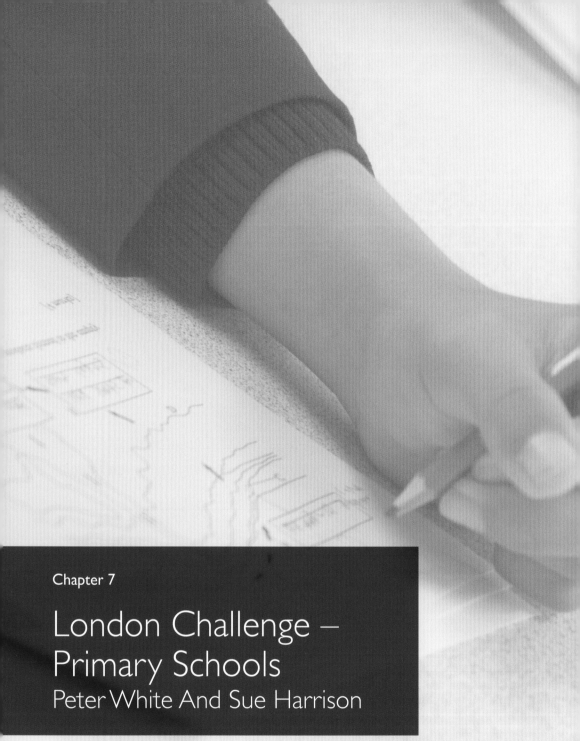

Chapter 7

London Challenge –
Primary Schools
Peter White And Sue Harrison

In 2006, after the very successful Keys to Success school improvement work in secondary schools, the London Challenge and The London Leadership Strategy (under the auspices of the National College for School Leadership) expanded its operation to include primaries. As with the secondary project, this used a coaching model where successful school leaders worked with leaders in schools identified (by their local authority and the Department for Education) as causing concern.

The initial work took root slowly. Two Support Consultants, both serving headteachers, were recruited by the National College. With the help of an excellent administrative team, they then set about recruiting other successful heads as Consultant Leaders. They sought out leaders with the ability to build relationships, empathise, prioritise but above all have the heart for helping to turn around a school in trouble (and at the same time, of course, maintain the quality and standards in their own school). The Support Consultants visited potential recruits in situ, interviewing both them and their colleagues as part of the vetting process and ensuring they had the capacity to support another school. This was followed by a Hay 360° assessment of the headteacher's leadership competencies. Once deemed suitable, the 20 new recruits were then rigorously trained in the ways of coaching. At this point, the Support Consultant carefully matched the Consultant Leader to their partner schools: never in the same local authority as their own, but geographically close enough to get to without too much difficulty. In 2010, Ofsted identified this careful matching of partners as being critical to success and further noted the importance of support coming *"without local strings attached and without conflicts of interest"* (Ofsted, 2010).

Matching done, it was early in 2007 when the first wave of primary 'System Leaders' were meaningfully deployed and their real work began. In the spirit of the pilot model, the initial brief was for the Consultant Leaders to win the confidence of the headteacher they were supporting. Although some had signed up for the experience, many colleagues in the supported schools were initially unwilling and/or bemused participants. Consultant Leaders used many a sensitive and creative ploy to win the trust of their headteacher partners. Once this was achieved (and often strong bonds established) there followed difficult coaching conversations and then practical help to support an action plan that would bring about improvements in leadership (at every level of the organisation) and consequently standards.

It was expected that to ensure sustainable change, this bespoke school-to-school work would take 18 months to two years to complete. It was not hard-edged but gently done – there was no 'naming and shaming' – it was an improvement model. Indeed, so positive were the relationships that a good number of the successfully supported headteachers later became Consultant Leaders themselves. The cost of the programme to taxpayers was minimal – supply cover and a consultancy fee to the Consultant Leader school – and this was, anyway, far outweighed by the results. It seemed then that the foundations were well laid to achieve The London Leadership Strategy's 2007 declared key objectives found in recruitment material for prospective Consultant Leader (author unknown):

- Raise standards for pupils in all London schools.

- Attract the best teachers and ensure their retention.

- Narrow the achievement gap within London schools.

- Support best/next practice gained from England and internationally.

- Promote London as a world leader in educational leadership through sharing the learning with others.

The first three objectives, grounded and business-like and the final two indicative of the innovative, cutting edge contributions to educational research and practice we had come to expect from the independent National College/London Leadership Strategy. By 2008, the latter objectives changed to be the more prosaic:

- Develop effective models of intervention to address challenges faced.

- Promote a culture of collegial, facilitated and sustained, rather than prescribed and dictated leadership development (Matthews, P., 2008).

Nothing succeeds like success! Though slowly evolved, the outcomes of the primary pilot drew the attention of policy makers who rightly saw huge potential in this emerging 'systems leadership' to the greater benefit of London's children and schools (after all, there are 1820 primary schools in London, some 300 of which in 2008 had Key Stage 2 results below floor targets and the initial project had touched but twenty of them). By 2008, Consultant Leaders had become Local Leaders of Education (LLE) and the National College began its campaign to recruit headteachers from outstanding schools across the country as National Leaders of Education (NLE). The London Challenge grew into City Challenge, the latest Support Consultant Leader changed his title to Director of the London Primary Team and Challenge Advisers for primary schools, with a three-year brief, were put in place by the DfE to direct operations. With only three years to show sustainable support and progress, a new urgency underpinned the work of the Challenge.

It is interesting that the 2010 Ofsted Report on the London Challenge only acknowledges the inclusion of primary schools into the scheme from 2008. Although seemingly insignificant, the early work described above was of no small consequence and led the way for the more critical and sharper focused interventions that were to follow. Now, with a considerably improved budget, the Challenge Advisers used performance data to identify an initial 60 London primary Keys to Success schools for the programme in its new incarnation, thus requiring the drafting in of 60 top quality LLEs. What had originally been a leisurely and very thorough recruitment process now became more frenzied. However, there was no doubting that the talent was out there: some of those 20 pioneering Consultant Leaders (now renamed LLEs) close to the end of their assignments were encouraged to make an early exit from the schools they were supporting; the existing team was implored to identify colleagues in their networks who might suit the LLE role; Ofsted reports were trawled for likely candidates and, with an attractive financial incentive, there were any number of takers and the target was quickly reached.

The Primary Strategy Team had grown to six, some of the new members recommended by the lead Challenge Adviser. Under its new Director, team members managed to visit every potential LLE to do at least a superficial screening to ensure suitability. There was at that time still emphasis on maintaining a coaching model of improvement and this presented another small dilemma: how to provide immediate and appropriate training to the newly-recruited LLEs? In the event, coaching skills training was delivered by the East Midlands Learning Centre in the first instance – this continued until there were sufficient numbers of (hastily trained) home-grown, London-based facilitators. Nonetheless, in order to respond to need, some LLEs were deployed before they had a chance to enjoy any training whatsoever.

It was this ability to 'act fast' using good local intelligence that became the trademark of the London Challenge post-2008. Once the initial demand had been met, the Primary Strategy Team continued the recruitment of LLEs and established a database of successful headteachers trained and ready to be deployed at a moment's notice. Each had been in headship for at least five years, had a track record of success, outstanding leadership qualities and a "passionate commitment to helping other schools… give young people a better deal" (Matthews P, 2008). Schools and indeed in some cases local education authorities, were regularly scrutinised by the Challenge Adviser and the numbers meeting the threshold for support grew and so it wasn't long before those LLEs in the 'pool' saw action.

As well as keeping numerous other, often harassing, professionals at bay, the LLEs' now more uncompromising role was to help their colleagues:

- Build capacity at every level in order to improve standards.

- Build sustainability so that repeated periods of support were unlikely.

- Develop shared values and consistency in practice across the school.

- Focus and be persistent in improving the deal for pupils.

- Grow a learning school.

- Have high expectations and a sense of urgency (slow and steady improvement is not enough).

In order to achieve this, some creativity was expected of the LLEs in brokering necessary support. Sometimes they had expertise to call on in their own school and their colleagues would work peer-to-peer in the supported school, sharing good practice and building capacity. Occasionally, the Challenge Advisers might be called upon to identify support from specialist consultants working outside the bounds of the London Challenge. However, where there was a repeated requirement for a particular intervention/support, Challenge Adviser engaged the talents of London practitioners to develop home-grown programmes in response to demand. In this way, packages such as 'Beyond Monitoring' and guides to quick wins like 'Maths – Achieving Levels 3, 4 and 5' contributed to rising standards in primary schools across London.

Most frequently, LLEs identified the key issue for the supported school as a deficiency in the quality of teaching and learning. Often, Keys to Success schools had few (or no) role models to demonstrate exemplary practice to those teachers with good potential. In these instances, the LLE would broker places on appropriate courses such as the Improving Teacher (ITP) and Outstanding Teacher Programmes (OTP). In order for the fix to be quick, The London Leadership Strategy ran these programmes almost continuously in venues across London. Ofsted reported in 2010 that in the first two years of the primary London Challenge, some 600 primary teachers had undertaken the Improving Teacher Programme (Ofsted, 2010). The programmes were hosted in schools graded 'good' and 'outstanding' by Ofsted and offered the opportunity for participants to see real lessons taught by exemplary practitioners.

Keys to Success schools were encouraged to send two, preferably three, participants so that together they could reflect upon and analyse what they had seen and learnt. In a survey of headteachers in the three City Challenge areas, "… the Outstanding Teacher Programme was the most highly-rated element of the Good to…(G2) programmes, identified as 'very effective' by two thirds of the G2 heads…" (Hutchings, M. et al, 2012). So it was with headteachers in the primary Keys to Success schools who, when asked to grade their colleagues before and after attending the courses, were consistently able to confirm a rise in the number of good and outstanding lessons they observed.

Whilst the hard data is now not easily accessible, it is true to say that the improvement in teaching practice amongst course participants was profound and made a great contribution to the overall improvement to standards. By 2010, Ofsted confirmed that "*(London Challenge) primary schools… are… improving rapidly… The contextual value-added measures of the participating schools… have risen significantly from below average in 2008 (99.566) to above average in 2010 (100.14)*" (Ofsted, 2010).

We cannot say to what degree this success can be attributed to the impact of Outstanding Teacher Programmes and Improving Teacher Programmes, but both courses and their contemporary offshoots (the 'Successful Teaching and Learning' programme, for example) are a legacy of the Challenge and are still available through the LLS, now a not-for-profit organisation run and led by serving headteachers and just as innovative as at its inception.

The quality of teaching having been secured, the Keys to Success schools began to shift their focus to learning and the outcomes for disadvantaged pupils in particular. Breaking the link between disadvantage and low attainment had always been a fundamental aim of the London Challenge. There was money available to fund innovative learning interventions that would raise attainment for the most vulnerable groups of children in our schools, in particular those eligible for Free School Meals (FSM) and all schools were invited to 'narrow the gap'. As well as offering training on how to effectively track pupil progress, LLEs were now brokering key skills programmes for their partners. Nationally recognised 'hub' schools sprung up to provide training on the successful application of these resources (for example, Department for Education programmes like *The Extra Mile* and *Gaining Ground*, or internationally successful ethos-changing approaches such as *Whatever it Takes*).

In their evaluation of the City Challenge programme, Hutchings et al asserted that "… *in all three Challenge areas the attainment gap in Keys to Success… primary schools narrowed by around 4%… This compares with a national 2.2% decrease in the Free School Meals attainment gap*".

With the additional funding (£3K per school) came a universal raised awareness of the Free School Meals gap in attainment; it gave further focus and impetus to sharing successful strategies school-to-school. It also occupied the attention of government and Ofsted, both of which used the success or not of narrowing the gap as a measure of school and leadership competency. The somewhat ad hoc funding was soon harnessed through identified grants and today we have the Pupil Premium to additionally finance the provision for children eligible for Free School Meals. Details of the Pupil Premium are in the public domain and schools have to justify how it is spent, the outcomes for pupils and the consequent closing of the attainment gap between those children eligible for Free School Meals and those not. Much research has gone in to determining the most effective interventions and the Sutton Trust has a dedicated toolkit that provides guidance to schools on the success of a variety of programmes and approaches.

Soon after the Challenge Advisers were appointed, there was a realisation that, whilst successful in the short-term, working 1:1 with schools would not necessary result in the enduring and significant change required to leave a sustainable legacy for the capital. Now that the culture of peer-to-peer support was firmly established, there was an imperative to 'grow the top' in order that there was a sufficient supply of willing talent to provide assistance to the most needy London schools once the project ended. In response, Challenge Advisers clustered willing schools into generously resourced Primary Challenge Groups. These triads of schools led by a good or outstanding school and facilitated by an LLE, identified a common priority for improving standards and were funded to work collaboratively and share expertise in the realisation of their goal. Interestingly, Street (2011) reported that there was a 'disconnect' between the role of the LLE in the groups and the focus of the training, which concentrated too much on coaching skills rather than on supporting school improvement.

However, it is clear that as a by-product of working in Primary Challenge Groups, the characteristics of good and outstanding leadership and practice rubbed off on individuals/ schools and further inroads were made in growing sustainable improvement at all levels of the organisations involved. By the end of the project in 2011, some 150 schools were involved in, and influenced by, working in Primary Challenge Groups. One assessment of the initiative showed that all the schools sampled were able to provide evidence of a positive impact on teaching and an NFER evaluation of Primary Challenge Groups reported that results had improved in all participating schools.

Many of the schools in the Primary Challenge Groups did indeed move from (Ofsted defined) 'satisfactory' to 'good' or from 'good' to 'outstanding' under the influence of the other schools in their association and/or through engagement with the programmes available from the London Challenge. As well as the ITP and OTP, a new programme emerged designed specifically to contribute to 'growing the top'. The Good to Great (G2G) experience targeted headteachers with the ambition and drive to become outstanding leaders. Whilst this work stream carried little financial incentive for participants, it had kudos and established powerful networks of headteachers and schools and so there was no lack of willing contributors. By the very nature of its make-up, this project was destined to be successful and many of the participants went on to be influential key players in delivering ever-improving standards in London's schools.

The increased confidence of the most successful headteachers proved an effective resource for local authorities, too. Faced with swinging budget cuts and a reduction in advisory and support personnel, the local authority turned to their talented local leaders to shore up their school improvement services. With the demise of Teachers' Centres and a reduction in professional development and training opportunities, the hub schools, some now accredited Teaching Schools, came in to their own. Innovative still, as well as being the nerve centre for implementing new government initiatives, they provide a plethora of opportunities for practitioners: from initial training to the development of Specialist Leaders of Education (SLE) charged with continuing the distinctive school-to-school work pioneered by the London Challenge.

In turn, former participants in the London Challenge sought to maintain the empowering partnerships that had been a signature strength of the original project. With impetus from The London Leadership Strategy, these self-starting and mutually beneficial, local and inter-borough networks sprung up countrywide, Challenge Partners (see page 131) being one such.

"*An important consequence of the London Challenge is that… school… (leaders) become influenced by the rigour and high expectations of… (working with their) colleagues… As a result teachers and their leaders begin to understand their own importance and value in providing effective education to London children. That sense of moral purpose is not often expressed to a region as a whole.*" (Ofsted, 2010). It would seem that this sense of moral purpose prevails.

The once panoramic view may now be fragmented, but whether or not the new perspective is to your liking, the London Challenge has undoubtedly contributed to the current educational landscape. Those who signed up to the vision recognised early on the significance of the work they were doing and the impact it had on changing the narrative of school improvement and changing the lives of London's children.

Chapter 8

The London Challenge: A Regional Model Of School System Reform And Improvement

Vanessa Ogden

Introduction

London education is complex and shifts constantly in response to political, social and economic change. As a place, London is subject to changes that forcefully affect its population, demography, economic growth and employment and, although ultimately the effects are felt everywhere, London's international and economic importance means that its success has implications for the whole country. This was a key reason why London's secondary schools became such a focus of attention in 2002. It was politically, socially and economically unacceptable that London should be the worst-performing region in the country and so a bespoke approach to system-wide school improvement was born: the London Challenge.

One of the reasons for the success of the London Challenge was its bespoke and flexible strategy, fit for purpose for the region and its schools. A tailored approach to school improvement is important. 'Place' affects education. The inter-relationship between a school and the 'place' where it is situated – its neighbourhood – is fundamental. The same is true for a system of schools. A school's region is also unique and so likewise, system-wide school improvement needs to be tailored to regions.

The London Challenge also taught us how the leadership of regional system-wide improvement could be configured most effectively. 'Top-down' strategy from central government does not create successful or lasting change in education because of the powerful role that practitioners play in education policy implementation. The London Challenge demonstrated how policy-makers and practitioners together can manage system reform successfully. Fundamentally, this depends on practitioner engagement within a 'high trust/high accountability' framework, where school leaders are trusted by government to lead change and to be accountable for delivering high standards.

This chapter explores what is needed in a regional strategy for system-wide school improvement like that of London to ensure that the best education is provided for every child.

The importance of regional context and the changing landscape of London

The London Challenge was introduced in late 2002 to address the under-performance of London's secondary schools compared to every other region in England. London had trailed behind other regions for many years and although when Labour took the office of government in 1997, many strategies were introduced including 'Excellence in Cities', they had little effect on London schools' performance. This is often overlooked in the recent discourse about the successes of London, as is the context of education in the capital at the time. Significant challenges existed in London socially, economically and demographically, which made it both a city of great advantage and of great inequity and these dynamics had a direct impact on London's schools.

Standards in schools in London varied considerably, often when they were within close proximity to each other. In Haringey in 2002, for example, pupils at Fortismere School achieved 67% 5+ A*-C, whereas those at White Hart Lane School (now Woodside High) achieved 24%. This was not including English and Maths, which was not measured at the time. In some schools, attainment was breathtakingly low. My first teaching post in 1993 was in a challenging school where only 9% of pupils achieved 5+ A*-C (not including English and Maths). When the London Challenge was launched 10 years later, things were not much better. There were 70 London secondary schools out of 407 where pupils attained less than 25% 5+ A*-C (not including English and Maths) or which were in an Ofsted category of 'special measures' or 'serious weaknesses'.

This was to do with a whole variety of educational problems within schools, including weak leadership, poor teaching and the struggle to find staff, particularly in schools where the challenges were greatest. London was not the place of choice in which to teach for most people and vacancies in teaching and leadership posts were high. Variation in school quality was exacerbated by this context and the difference in standards between schools reflected to a significant extent London's socio-economic context and its increasing social polarisation.

London's economy had importance for the success of the whole country and so it drew constant attention. By the 1990s, however, this decline had reversed and there were important economic and social changes which affected London schools:

- *Changes in the type of employment available and for which schools were preparing young people.* Finance, business, public service work, the creative and media industries and ICT were all areas of growth. Employment in these sectors required higher levels of qualification, especially at graduate level and schooling had not kept pace with this.

- *Changes in economic growth, which were distributed inequitably.* This affected communities in London differentially. Salaries varied considerably, worklessness rates in London were higher than anywhere else and concentrated in specific neighbourhoods and there was a high rate of child poverty.

- *Changes in population, which were significant.* Economic migration increased leading to greater ethnic diversity in London's school population. Hall remarked in his 2007 study 'London Voices, London Lives' that "*London has a demographic profile quite unlike any other part of the country; it is almost like a different country*" (Hall 2007:7).

In 2002, London was a more populous, much wealthier, more diverse city than it had been. It was a city of greater opportunity – but it was also a city of greater inequality. Salary differential and housing affordability, together with a very good public transport system, conspired to create a dynamic in London's secondary school system which fuelled social polarisation and exacerbated the variation in standards between schools. School choice and perceptions about the relative merits of different schools became related to social division.

Moving house to a different area, paying for schooling or using London's extensive transport system to travel some distance had an effect on the schools themselves and the neighbourhoods where they were situated. Those that could afford to do so moved house thus creating a rise in property prices and in consequence, selecting out those with less advantages. This is sometimes described as a 'postcode effect'. As the neighbourhood demographic changes, so does the character of the school that serves it. This is because there is an intricate relationship between a school and where it is situated. Neighbourhood disadvantage makes good schooling harder to achieve since attainment is related to social advantage and so context becomes a driver for school quality.

The situation in London had to be addressed given the capital's importance in the national economy. Schools needed to respond to the social and economic changes that had taken place but, given the difficulties which they were facing, they could not do it alone. Not only was a significant culture change required within London's schools they also needed help to deal with the context they were facing and this required complex and multi-layered strategy.

Those that established the London Challenge recognised the need for a context-dependant strategy for the region from the outset. Estelle Morris had already decided in the embryonic stages of the policy that a special approach was needed. A dinner was held at the Royal Society of Arts in the autumn of 2002 which was attended by key practitioners in London. The theme was 'What was unique and special about London?'

Drawing upon such discussions, as well as a great deal of contextual research and visits to many London secondary schools, the London Challenge team, led by Jon Coles, set about the creation of bespoke initiatives that were calibrated to London's needs. They developed a deep knowledge of the London school environment and acted reflexively to changes in the system as incremental improvements occurred. This was critical to the policy's effectiveness. It allowed the London Challenge to evolve over time as the school system matured and capacity increased.

Research on school improvement in challenging circumstances has shown that effective leadership which brings about change is linked to sophisticated skills in the interpretation of context and the ability to be reflexive and adaptable in response. This was true of the London Challenge. The 2003 policy text brought together into what Coles described as a "coherent gestalt" a number of pre-existing policy initiatives such as: 'Extended Schools' to focus community regeneration around schools; school specialism to create renewed leadership and direction; key worker loans for housing to keep teachers in London; the Leadership Incentive Grant to improve leadership capacity; and Teach First to improve teacher supply. Brighouse commented in an interview that it was almost as though "everyone's favourite policy was there". However, it was the intelligent and co-ordinated calibration of these initiatives for each school context that was important and the London Challenge team's leadership of the strategy, which allowed the consultant headteachers to get on with their work below the political radar by developing the Keys to Success initiative and The London Leadership Strategy. This latter point is significant.

In the 2003 policy text, which is 'top-down' in character and reflective of central government's more controlling approach to school improvement, the Keys to Success initiative and The London Leadership Strategy had little prominence. Yet the policy text of 2010, *Lessons Learned From London: Secondary School Improvement Programmes* presented a very different picture of the London Challenge than that of 2003. In the 2003 text, for example, there was no reference to The London Leadership Strategy. The description in the policy proposals of school leadership development in London was confined to some general comments about the need to develop headship and middle leadership roles, together with some proposals for the establishment of a London Centre for leadership and some commitment to additional financial resourcing for this. By contrast in 2010, the strategy for leadership development had become an entity in itself known as The London Leadership Strategy: serving practitioners were leading the school improvement system in London and creating transformation from within. The London Challenge had evolved to become a strategy for self-sustaining, system-wide improvement that was driven by practitioners who were at the cutting edge of innovation and achievement.

The shift from top-down control to practitioner leadership was not accidental. Brighouse knew that practitioners' buy-in to the London Challenge would be critical to its success. This was partly to do with the nature of education policy. Also, it was to do with context. There needed to be a bed-rock of support for the policy from within the field of practice given the competitive nature of London's school system at the time. School leaders would need to step across the divide and work together to support each other. Creating this culture change required purposeful leadership and co-ordination.

The leadership and management of London's system reform

Policy is implemented – or not – within the context of practice and in education policy, practitioners have a relatively powerful position. Educators often act alone in their work – for example a teacher in a classroom or a headteacher determining which aspects of a policy should be implemented – and so there is fairly wide-ranging professional autonomy. As a result, a policy can be distorted, subverted or ignored by those responsible for enacting it, usually practitioners. This has given rise to a whole set of policy levers in education designed either to curb or incentivise certain kinds of behaviours amongst school leaders and teachers, for example through performance measures, inspection or statutory requirement.

Even so, headteachers remain important gatekeepers of policy implementation in schools. Without their active support for the policy, the London Challenge team knew it would not be successful. A strategy for leading the reform of London's school system which engaged practitioners (both headteachers and teachers) willingly in the challenges of change was required. Fullan argues in a number of his works on system leadership the importance of co-ordination in sustained, widespread system reform, saying that "*There is no getting around it. For the entire system to move, you need relentless, resolute leadership from the top*" (Fullan 2010:13 – 14). Collaboration between schools within the competitive London context of the time had to be actively managed. There were two complementary forms of system leadership in the London Challenge that allowed this to happen.

First was the figurehead leadership of the Chief Advisor for London Schools. In the first few years, this position was held by Tim Brighouse, a strong and trusted leader in education who located himself visibly within the field of practice and who had a track record of success in inner city schooling. To achieve the kind of system reform that was needed, he had to engage directly with practitioners from whom as figurehead he could otherwise be remote. As has been mentioned, a deep understanding of the context for reform in London and its history was important but he also had to find a way to achieve what he regarded as a "prime purpose" – "*securing a strong and widely shared commitment to the highest common factor of the organisational purpose and values*" (Brighouse 2005:114). It required two things: close communication with practitioners, despite his remote position, and commitment from them to a vision of how things could be better in London.

As a remote leader (as Tim Brighouse references in his earlier chapter), he recognised the importance of every single communication with individual practitioners. Not only did he set out to meet headteachers and teachers at every possible opportunity, he went as far as to write letters to individual practitioners whom he met, thanking them for an aspect of work which he had particularly noticed. These letters were handwritten – there are London practitioners who have them still. Also important was the vision that Tim Brighouse described and the language that he used. In *Passionate Leadership in Education* (Davies and Brighouse 2008), he discussed the notion of 'skald', the Norwegian word for the eloquent poet who told stories of past, glorious success on the eve of or during the course of an expedition. Stories of success create energy and when beginning a culture change such as that which was needed in London, Brighouse set about it through the use of supportive, affirming and speculative language, finding those with a 'can-do' philosophy and using their impetus to further develop and implement the vision. It turned attention away from the stories that reinforced failure such as those that had prevailed about London to a vision of something greater. It created hope – hope that one could be part of a better future for London.

Hope is an important part of education. One needs a 'utopian imagination' in schools, especially where the challenges are greatest. Teaching and school leadership are premised on hope – the hope that there will have been an improvement after one has carried out one's work. Thus many London practitioners responded to a utopian vision of how things could be better. As Jon Coles stated in his interview for my doctoral research: "*People strive to be part of something that is greater than themselves.*" A vision for London, founded upon powerful ideals about how things could be better – one that seemed to proclaim the establishment of 'a new heaven and a new earth' in London – had a transformative effect on London practitioners, their morale and their belief in what was possible.

The moral purpose which was expressed within that vision was a potent, unifying and driving force for practitioners. Michael Fullan has pointed out that "*Most teachers want to make a difference and they especially like leaders who help them and their colleagues achieve success in terrible circumstances*" (Fullan 2011: 4). He goes on to argue that moral purpose cannot be intention only: it has to be genuine and it has to be enacted. Importantly, practitioners in London got behind the London Challenge because they could see it was authentic. Not only was it founded in Brighouse's own commitment to social justice and the importance of education as a means of achieving it, they could see even before the policy was launched, the start of a raft of work on school-to-school support by a small group of serving headteachers, who were committed to standing 'shoulder-to-shoulder' with others they were supporting and to be jointly accountable for the outcomes. This brings the discussion to the second form of system leadership in the London Challenge – team leadership.

Remote leaders cannot work alone within a regional system. If success was really going to take root in London for the long term, others needed to share the leadership and so Tim Brighouse worked in partnership with a team of people who became known as the London Challenge team. The team was a small group of people which included policy-makers such as the Minister for London Schools Stephen Twigg, a small number of civil servants, eight London Challenge Advisors and six consultant headteachers. This team sat behind the figurehead leadership of the Chief Advisor for London Schools, looking after the appointment, matching and deployment of consultant headteachers and quality assuring their work. It acted as the 'system glue' of the London Challenge through what Michael Fullan delineates as their "constant communication with all groups", their "precision-based capacity building and problem-solving strategies" and their "careful recruitment of leaders" (Fullan 2011:47). As the London Challenge evolved, the team became the central infrastructure of the work of the London Challenge, leading its development and ensuring that capacity for future leadership was built into the system.

Meeting weekly at the Department for Education, the London Challenge team co-ordinated the work of the London Challenge, analysing the data on schools across London as it changed and responding accordingly and taking responsibility for a number of leadership activities, which were fundamental to the policy's success:

- The bespoke, personalised, context-dependent approach to improvement for each school.

- The matching process between headteachers and their schools based on a wide range of intelligence about respective leadership styles, the contexts of each school and their relative strengths.

- The brokering process which was a hard-edged approach by contract and based on mutual accountability.

- The quality assurance of the work through direct accountability to ministers via the team.

In a system that, in 2003 when the London Challenge was launched, suffered from weak leadership capacity, the high-level expertise and experience of those who were part of the London Challenge team were essential. The intellectual prowess of those who formed the team and their moral commitment gave considerable legitimacy to the London Challenge and the credibility of their work was fundamentally important to the policy's success. In particular, the management of the contractual process, which the London Challenge team controlled and the advice and guidance they offered to the consultant headteachers when situations sometimes became tricky were crucial. Otherwise, consultant headteachers were trusted to act autonomously to create a bespoke programme of support tailored to each school and to develop other headteachers to become consultants. In this way, through coaching and knowledge transfer, the London Challenge built leadership capacity within the system – capacity which still exists more than four years on.

As a result of the leadership approach of the London Challenge team, practitioners increasingly engaged with the policy over time and capacity in the system increased incrementally year on year. By the time the London Challenge finished, it was led entirely by serving or recently serving headteachers under the figurehead leadership of David Woods, previously the lead London Challenge Advisor, and it had a rather different relationship to central government than in 2003. A school-led system had emerged in London.

The London Challenge and school-led system transformation

In the 1980s and 1990s, the policy framework for education was centrally driven and exerted a controlling force on the field of practice. However, as rapid improvement became evident as a result of the work of the consultant headteachers and London Challenge advisors, the relationship between policy-makers and practitioners gradually altered. The London Challenge became the expression of Fullan's longed goal for system leadership – the bringing together of the two separate worlds of policy-maker and practitioner.

In interview, Stephen Twigg stated that policy-makers began to realise as time went on during the London Challenge that previous approaches needed to change and so the environment was ripe for a new way of envisioning education policy-making. The days of 'command and control' and 'top-down government' with 'bottom-up initiative' were no longer suitable for the new super-complex social terrain of the 21st century and so the role of government was to provide the right conditions for practitioners to lead policy development. As Bangs et al have pointed out: "*Government policy-making is most likely to be effective when it is shaped by the principle that a government's role should be to provide the conditions for change rather than trying to legislate the behaviour*" (Bangs et al 2011: 181). Thus, Coles, who led the policy team at the Department for Education, eventually took the view that his role was "*about giving people the space, the structures and the support – and to create a culture in which they can do this, so they can do it for themselves*" (Ogden 2012:120).

The way in which this was achieved by the policy-makers in the London Challenge team such as Coles and Twigg, was to set a framework of conditions for 'high accountability', which focused rigorously on standards of performance. The success of the consultant headteachers was measured through improvements in schools' key performance indicators such as GCSE results and Ofsted inspection judgements. Coles, Twigg and other government representatives created the expectations, the accountability structure and systems of regular feedback whilst trusting the practitioners in the team, eventually giving them the autonomy to set the initiatives and strategy themselves through which improvement would happen. Through this 'high trust, high accountability framework', the policy-makers and practitioners in the London Challenge team established what David Hopkins has described as a 'creative tension'. They became co-constructors of the policy and consequently, the London Challenge achieved the transition from national prescription to professionalism, which Hopkins has described as the desired aim of system reform: "*Transition from 'prescription' to 'professionalism' is not easy to achieve. In order to move from one to the other, strategies are required that not only continue to raise standards but also develop social, intellectual and organisational capacity*" (Hopkins 2012: 167).

Between 2003 – when the London Challenge was officially launched – and 2010 – when the policy quietly ended – leadership capacity was systematically built until the London Challenge became an exemplar of system leadership in its fullest expression. The London Challenge team and the consultant headteachers who worked with it developed the social, intellectual and organisational capacity to achieve this, built incrementally and carefully in a sustained way through the school improvement model that was constructed, the vision and values that were created and the infrastructure and team leadership which was established to direct the policy's work. Thus a system was created and governed in which school leaders led self-sustaining school improvement in London as well as becoming leaders of system reform, co-constructing policy alongside government.

There was something more within the work of the London Challenge which is important to note about its particular approach to system leadership. There was significant power invested in the Consultant Leaders of the London Challenge through their status as NLE, leader of system reform and co-constructor of policy. Although literature on system leadership refers often to the need for moral purpose on the part of system leaders, there is little to suggest where it might come from and how one might avoid its corruption. The potential for 'knavery' (self-interested rather than public-spirited behaviour) and predatory behaviour amongst school leaders is a real one.

What the London Challenge team created to deal with this was a set of expectations concerning the social, intellectual and organisational capacities required of individuals, as well as the system. Consultant headteachers were expected to conform to a set of values, skills and behaviours, which were present in the shared language of the London Challenge team, its training and its literature. Whilst not explicitly set out by the London Challenge in a coherent code of conduct for individual system leaders, they can be traced in the way in which the team operated and talked about the policy. In setting them out here, I have referred to other theorists' writing where there is wider evidence than just the London Challenge of the importance of each one. They were:

- The expression of moral purpose: moral purpose sat at the core of the London Challenge's work. It was about "raising the bar and closing the gaps in terms of student learning and achievement" (Hopkins 2007: 9). It also included a commitment to issues of wider social justice and the desire to break down economic and social barriers for students and commit societies to investment in young people.

- The commitment to schools other than their own through taking responsibility, which includes – but which is greater than – accountability: the London Challenge took responsibility for the educational well-being of all pupils within the region in which they worked or amongst a group of schools with which they worked. They were not just accountable – they stood alongside their colleagues in other schools and shared the responsibility for the achievement of all.

- The requirement to develop a more sophisticated set of behaviours, capabilities and skills in leadership than are required in single school leadership: London Challenge Consultant Leaders were required to have 'adaptive' skills, reflexive behaviours that could engage with an extensive range of diverse people and ways of strategic thinking that could respond to a wide number of contexts.

- The desire and capacity to develop and regenerate whole communities through learning and achievement: London Challenge Consultant Leaders had to be prepared to take on a variety of roles to transform communities, engaging all stakeholders in support of regeneration through learning.

These values, skills and behaviours permeated the work of the London Challenge team and the consultant headteachers as they strived together for system-wide improvement. In many ways, they present a framework for professional conduct in school-led system reform, which is important where the mediating role of the consultant headteacher at the interface with policy has such power and autonomy. In a competitive system, the potential for perverse incentives to operate at the expense of children (albeit unintentionally) is very strong and so school-led system reform must find a way to mitigate this.

In conclusion, this chapter has made a number of points about school-led system reform.

First, a regional approach is important. This is not an argument for a return to local authority control. Regions need to be both big enough to provide an effective data context on performance and to bring experienced, successful leaders together to support schools in need and small enough to allow for good local intelligence and swift response. Any regional approach must also be bespoke – tailored to fit social, economic and political context. Simply lifting the London Challenge and implementing the strategies as they were for London is unlikely to be fully effective. Borrowing and innovating based on what has been learned from London is much more likely to be successful.

Second, leadership and co-ordination of regional system-wide school reform is essential. Figurehead leadership provides the inspiration and force to galvanise support for the strategy from practitioners and policy-makers. The team leadership enacts the strategy, directing and quality assuring its work and ensuring faithfulness to vision and values. The central brokering, matching and deployment processes, as well as good regional intelligence and the ability to respond quickly in a crisis are all important components of successful regional co-ordination.

Third, the engagement of practitioners in support of system-wide school reform is crucial and this happens most effectively when:

- A vision is created for what the strategy is setting out to achieve, accompanied by narrative and metaphor and founded in an authentic and passionate commitment to social justice.

- A corporate allegiance to the vision and its values is established, together with a regional identity that can build networks of professional support and development.

Fourth, school-led system reform requires a framework of high accountability within which school leaders can have the trust of policy-makers and the autonomy to create the right strategies for improvement. Those strategies should be designed to build the social, intellectual and organisational capacity for system-wide improvement. They should include: leadership, regional infrastructure and systems for engagement. Importantly, they should also include clearly defined expectations governing the individual professional values and behaviours of system leaders to support the preservation of moral purpose in the system.

Policy-making often has a short memory. It is easy to forget from where London has come in terms of school improvement and that for many schools that have made progress in the past decade, there is still fragility. It is right to focus on other areas of the country where there are challenges – rural or coastal, for example – and for London to share its learning and to have a reciprocal relationship with other regions. For example, The London Leadership Strategy, now as an independent not-for-profit organisation set up by those involved in the London Challenge, is currently working alongside colleagues in Somerset supporting the practitioner-driven 'Somerset Challenge' and also the Norfolk partnership. The challenges for London schools have not gone away, though, in spite of the success. London still requires dedicated, regional attention, otherwise we risk the gains that have been made. The stakes will always be high in the capital given its context and this should not be forgotten.

Chapter 9

The Legacy Of The London Challenge

David Woods And Tim Brighouse

We are writing this almost four years after the official close of the London Challenge.

We intend it as an honest record of some of those who took part in the Challenge. Inevitably witnesses, of whom we are two, provide their own perceptions, backed by records kept but rely partly on memory. So we would not claim it as a completely accurate record, nor is it a full record of the many small and large interventions which were carried out during the period 2002-2011. We are aware, too, that the Challenge spent the whole period attending to secondary schools and just the last four years to primary schools: that is evident from reading the original prospectus and explains why in this account words like 'student' crop up rather more frequently than 'pupil'.

Although four years have passed since the London Challenge programme formally ended, its spirit lives on. One of the strongest features has been the way that the Challenge captured the hearts and minds of London schools and educators, united under a common goal to ensure that every child and young person thrived regardless of their background. The language, culture and DNA of the challenge appears to have been imprinted to an unusual degree on London's educational community. The following are among its features:

- A compelling and inclusive moral purpose and moral capital with strong, shared values, principles and beliefs.

- System leadership through expert school leaders designing strategies and brokering solutions, as well as directly supporting other schools in strengthening leadership and teaching.

- An unrelenting focus on raising standards and 'closing gaps' between groups of schools and pupils so that all children and young people stand a better chance of realising more of their potential.

- Collaboration, partnership working and practitioner networks sharing best practice through a range of activities, programmes and publications.

- Well-mobilised intellectual, social and organisational capital maintaining vision, energy, depth and staying power to produce excellent educational outcomes.

Outcomes have been transformed since the days when London was the lowest-performing region in the country. The three tests set in 2002 to raise attainment, to close gaps and to increase the percentage of good and outstanding schools have been met to the point where London is now the top performing region in the country, a position sustained in the

Our Regional Partnerships

LLS Regional Partnerships:

O London

O Medway

O Norfolk

O Poole

O Somerset

O South Gloucestershire

years after the Challenge. This transformation in outcomes is an educational phenomenon with significant profound implications for driving social mobility. A focus simply on regional headlines runs the danger of underplaying the true scale of London's turnaround for its most disadvantaged students, for it is here where the gap between London and the rest of the country is most evident. That demographics and deprivation are not necessarily destiny, so far as socio-economically disadvantaged youngsters are concerned, has been clearly demonstrated by London's schools, which have shown the difference that high quality leadership and teaching coupled with high expectations can make. The London Challenge succeeded in changing the narrative and mindsets so that 'better' is always possible within a culture of continuous school improvement.

The London Leadership Strategy

The London Leadership Strategy (LLS) was an essential part of the Challenge, as evidenced by Sue John in an earlier chapter. In 2011, this became a formally established Trust as the successor body to the London Challenge, chaired by David Woods and with headteachers from all phases acting as Directors. The LLS continues to connect and inspire schools in London under the leadership of senior heads who worked as part of the Challenge taking forward the major strategies, programmes and best practices, adapting them to the changing educational landscape. Every year at primary, special and secondary levels, London schools continue to access a variety of programmes and conferences run by the LLS such as *Securing Good, Good to Great, Going for Great* etc. The programmes and conferences support schools at different points of their improved journey within a framework of Teaching Schools, National Leaders of Education, Local Leaders of Education, Specialist Leaders of Education, and Lead Practitioners, offering bespoke support and challenge.

The LLS does not work in isolation but has developed some key strategic partnerships with other organisations striving to improve schools both within and outside London – notably Challenge Partners, Teach First and the Mayor with the Greater London Authority (GLA). The Challenge Partners organisation grew out of the London Challenge with many London heads at the forefront and now has some 350 schools in the country practising a quality assurance peer review model to drive forward a school-led, self-improving process. Teach First, which first took mostly in London, continues to thrive. It now places approximately 1,500 participants per year across the country with around 800 in London schools. Many of the programme's participants remain teaching in London, some of them now leading London's schools. The Mayor and the GLA have built on the legacy of the London Challenge to develop a London curriculum, a Lead Gold Club (representing best practice) and a range of learning hubs and conferences mobilising and sharing knowledge.

Sharing best practice beyond London

There are a growing number of area-based improvement strategies that to varying extents have taken inspiration from the London Challenge's methods and approach. Some of these are working in close partnership with The London Leadership Strategy, which is actively working to take the lessons learnt from London to the regions, including work with primary and secondary schools in Norfolk, Poole, Portsmouth, Somerset and South Gloucestershire, amongst others. Ongoing London Challenge programmes that run throughout England, as well as research in to what has worked historically, enables them to do this through peer-to-peer support and evidence-based practice.

The key factors of success regionally as disseminated by the London Challenge include:

- Developing a new sense of regional identity, which crosses jurisdictions and unlocks the potential of the wider community. This includes shared values and common goals.

- Changing the narrative, developing the culture – and high aspirations, across all disciplines and phases.

- Greater knowledge and dissemination of best practice.

- Effective school-to-school support with the capacity to confront problems and deliver solutions.

- A small, central resource that ensures rich knowledge is mobilised effectively. All school-to-school support is effectively brokered, leveraging in other agencies such as universities, businesses and other partnerships – to gain additional support in schools.

This process allows for effective knowledge of support and challenge, harnessing Teaching Schools and their alliances; NLEs, National Support Schools, Local Level SLEs, specialist level SLEs and excellent practitioners on a wider scale and at all levels.

The London Challenge shows us that it is possible to drive collaboration between schools in different localities, cutting across traditional local authority boundaries and exposing educational leaders and school support staff to great practice, beyond their normal frame of reference, which in turn opens up a wider pool of knowledge.

The regional challenge programmes in such places as Somerset and Norfolk are already starting to create a shared language and brand that educators can unite behind and they are welcoming external challenges and support from The London Leadership Strategy and other institutions. As these Regional Challenges continue to develop rapidly, alongside the DfE's Regional Commissioners of Education and Ofsted's regional structure, the architecture of the London Challenge provides an appropriate framework for success and can help to build a powerful momentum for future successful change.

It would be easy to end this short book on such a note of optimism – and of course we would never want to deny the essential importance in schools of creating a climate of hope, energy and enthusiasm among staff and students! Moreover, we do not wish to qualify in any way our essential message that 'cultural change in and among schools' requires the following features, all present in the London Challenge:

- A strong moral purpose as to what we are trying to achieve and to which all can easily subscribe.

- The use of language and actions which are at one with that moral purpose.

- A shared map of the processes of school improvement.

- The encouragement of school-to-school support and partnerships.

- A tireless commitment to learning more about teaching, learning, assessing and the other school improvement processes.

- Getting the right people in the right places, doing the right things at the right time, in the right way.

We intended this account, however, to be one from which others should learn, so some cautionary words are necessary. First and most obviously, not everything we attempted was successful. For example, some schools 'waxed' and then 'waned' during the London Challenge and that was down to not having the 'right people in the right place, doing the right things at the right time, in the right way'. There are some schools in some places that require extraordinary leadership, not merely to secure improvement but to sustain it: and we didn't always achieve that. Moreover, there were some parts of the prospectus for the London Challenge which appear to us to have been more successful than others and we have tried to point those out.

Secondly, a partnership working among schools is remarkably difficult to sustain and requires systemic support, which isn't yet thought through coherently within our educational system.

Thirdly, there is the obvious linked question of for how long can the 'London Challenge Effect' be sustained? After all, if schools can 'wax' and 'wane', so can whole schooling systems. Our view would be that a school-led system cannot be indefinitely sustained without some strategic overview, some glue to hold partnerships of schools together and sufficient resources to secure a sufficient supply of suitably qualified school staff. We know from the history of London's schools in, for example, the 1970s and 80s that city schools can very quickly decline. We believe that pan London oversight is essential and that the Mayor and the GLA are well placed to provide that working with the London local authorities.

As we said at the beginning, we decided to put our recollections on paper because the London Challenge has received so much attention – particularly in the years after its ending. Doubtless this has something to do with the increased attention to evidence-based policy making, fuelled partly by the establishment of the Education Endowment Foundation (EEF), funded by government and supported by the Sutton Trust and partly by the increased attention given at school level both to the EEF 'toolkit' of the comparative value of different popular interventions in schooling and by John Hattie's 'Visible learning'. The attention given to the London Challenge is at two levels of policy making, namely beyond the school (where it focuses on what central government, local authorities or chains can do to bring about school improvement in a period when school-to school support is regarded as a promising way to secure such school improvement) and at the level of the school itself.

As we said in the introduction, those making policy too often simply lift and transfer from one context to another. We reiterate that reading Nancy Cartwright and Jeremy Hardie's book *Evidence-Based Policy Making; A Practical Guide To Making It Better* seems to us an essential first step in trying to avoid some of the all too frequent mistakes made by those guiding the school system as a whole. Too often they ignore what those two authors call the 'vertical' and 'horizontal' subtle differences of context. What worked in Birmingham did not transfer exactly to London. What worked in London will not transfer exactly to Somerset, Norfolk or the North East: still less is there one answer for every school within those areas. Indeed at the level of the school itself, Nick Cowen and Nancy Cartwright have produced a very short 24 page booklet *Making The Most Of The Evidence In Education: A Guide For Working Out What Works… Here And Now.* Its last two sentences could be a fitting note on which to end this postscript: "*Deciding whether an intervention will work, or is working, requires professional judgement, preferably in the context of free and open discussion among colleagues. Direct evidence shows what works only for the context and populations actually studied*".

In London, we were lucky to have teachers and school leaders who shared a determination that all youngsters could and would succeed and that disadvantage beyond the school would not be mirrored within it. The London Challenge reinforced this determination and built upon it. They were willing to embrace any change of practice that would help them achieve success for their youngsters and their staff. We passionately believed what we were about and they knew we returned that respect for their skill, effort and practice and that together we could do something that would make others scratch their heads and ask 'Well how did they do that?'.

At least in that we succeeded. Far more importantly, the teachers and school leaders raised their game and changed the life chances of so many children and young people.

C.P. CAVAFY – ITHAKA

As you set out for Ithaka

hope the voyage is a long one,

full of adventure, full of discovery,

Laistrygonians and Cyclops,

angry Poseidon – don't be afraid of them:

you'll never find things like that on your way

as long as you keep your thoughts raised high,

as long as a rare excitement

stirs your spirit and body.

...

Hope the voyage is a long one.

May there be many a summer morning when,

with what pleasure, what joy,

you come into harbors seen for the first time;

...

Keep Ithaka always in your mind.

Arriving there is what you are destined for.

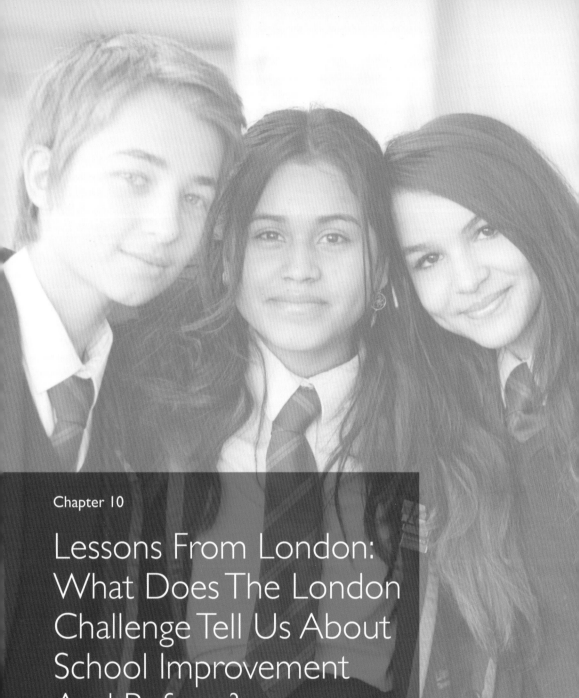

Chapter 10

Lessons From London: What Does The London Challenge Tell Us About School Improvement And Reform?

Chris Husbands

In her account of urban school reform, Kathryn McDermott makes the point that "within many cities, there are effective classrooms – 'beacon' schools and even clusters of such schools – but there are few if any examples of a successful model being expanded to the scope of an entire district" (McDermott, 2000: 83). The experience of London between 2003 and 2012 provides such an example. There have always been good schools and great teachers in London. Indeed, as some of the commentators on the London Challenge have pointed out, London has always enjoyed some striking educational advantages: a vibrant, if uneven economy; a ready supply of enthusiastic young teachers keen to begin their careers in the capital's schools and some real demographic advantages. But it also exemplifies many of the challenges facing urban school improvers: extremes of wealth and poverty; large areas of inadequate housing; a large, poorly paid service economy and high levels of intra-urban population mobility. If London has advantages, it also faces all the challenges, which face cities across the world. The achievement of the London Challenge is not that it secured school improvement: there have always been effective and improving schools in challenging settings, but rather that it provided a model for a comprehensive approach to school improvement across a complex, rapidly changing, economically unequal city.

Urban school improvement is tough. Charles Payne's compelling account of American school reform – *So Much Reform, So Little Change* – is subtitled "the persistence of failure in urban schools" – a reminder that despite repeated initiatives and innovations, for too long too many children have been failed by schools in large, economically divided cities. Payne is dismissive of reform which is disconnected from the daily realities of urban schools, dismissive of grand theories of change and concludes that "*there is no one lever we can move which will give us the purchase we need*" (Payne, 2008: 47). Payne argues that successful reform depends on what he calls "five fundamentals": instructional leadership, professional capacity, establishing a learning climate, family and community involvement and the quality of instruction. Moreover, successful school reform is "comprehensive, sustained and intense". Payne's book ends with a coruscating denunciation of what he calls "liberal and conservative theories of school reform" – the one arguing that school reform is impossible without serious assaults on poverty and the circumstances which create failure and the other that circumstances do not matter, that incentive structures alone can drive change. Both, he argues are extremely damaging to children. In practice, says Payne, we know a great deal about successful reform and he concludes his book with a motto for successful reform: "*No matter where in the social structure children are coming from, act as if their possibilities are boundless*".

This is the context against which we should think about the London Challenge: the context of taking school reform to scale. By the mid-1990s, the school effectiveness literature had spawned a strong tradition of school improvement practice. The challenges and techniques of school improvement were well disseminated. The importance of instructional leadership, of strong visionary management and careful improvement planning were well embedded. The techniques required to establish basic effectiveness and to begin improvement journeys in the most challenging of contexts were clear. But as individual schools improved and as successful headteachers of those schools were, rightly, lauded, the challenge of system improvement became more pressing.

It is always possible for individual schools to improve by – either by accident or design – subtly altering their intake or shifting their relationships with neighbouring schools. In the long run, all this does is to move failure around the system. It is not a recipe for serious or sustained improvement. Sustained improvement – improvement for all – needs something else: it needs systemic improvement. At the end of the 1990s and in the first decade of the present century, policy-makers became interested in taking school improvement to scale. Michael Fullan, quick to catch the improvement zeitgeist, commented in 1999, "*large-scale reform has returned, with a vengeance*". Writing in 2003, Lorna Earl and her colleagues noted that "*governments everywhere have moved education to centre stage, using policy levers to signal their intentions to improve education*". This sort of comprehensive school improvement – moving improvement from some schools to many in order to have regional or national impact on outcomes for young people has proved to be a huge challenge for policy-makers. What does London tell us about school improvement and reform?

Over the past two decades, several different models for large-scale reform have emerged globally. Pasi Sahlberg has characterised one of them as the 'GERM': the global education reform movement, characterised by a reliance on standardised testing, assessment-led reform and marketised deregulation – a market-led approach to reform which sees competition, within a strongly managed overall market, as the route to improvement. A second model sees system reform as being delivered by highly directive and centralised mandating of curriculum and pedagogic practices and is often said to characterise the successful systems of the Pacific Rim, systems that operate in settings where there are high levels of consensus about the value of education amongst almost all groups in society. A third model has been described as a 'tri-level' approach to improvement, which involves the careful alignment of national, regional and school improvement levers. It is underpinned by what Michael Fullan called the 'moral drive for improvement': a compelling vision of change and success for all learners.

As this book has demonstrated, the London Challenge was a concerted, if always pragmatic, collection of interventions designed to improve London schools, which depended on the co-ordination of action at several levels: it was central government which forced the pace of academisation on some local authorities; it was central government which, across tiers of municipal administration, provided the funding. Local government was not bypassed and local authorities played a significant role. And action was mobilised at school level, most importantly through the packages of support and school-to-school improvement plans which were developed across London. The latter was underpinned by one of the London Challenge's most elegant and least celebrated achievements: the generation of detailed performance and contextual data on London, grouping the 400 secondary schools into 23 'families' and later 'families' for primary schools. All this was, as the studies here have made plain, held together – led – by strong visionary leadership, building a vision of what London could be, holding onto optimism about what could be achieved whilst chivvying partners along. The argument is now often made that the London Challenge saw the emergence of a school-to-school approach to improvement and it is certainly true that in the later stages of the London Challenge, school leaders themselves drove the initiative, particularly through The London Leadership Strategy. But whilst school-led improvement was necessary, it seems to me that it is not sufficient to explain the success: the London Challenge needed the other – 'tri-level' ingredients: support from government and local visionary leadership. What characterised the success of the London Challenge was a willingness to try things out; to change direction at short notice when interventions were not succeeding and to combine interventions in ways which might work – but all within the framework of vertical co-operation between national, municipal and local levels and a commitment to mobilising schools collectively to improve outcomes for young people, wherever they happened to be educated.

The London Challenge was a set of policy interventions which evolved and changed over time. Collectively, the impact on attainment and performance was impressive, but as some studies have pointed out it was not universal – some parts of London improved faster than others. Partly as a result, it is difficult to identify which initiatives were the most successful. Different actors, perhaps drawing on hindsight, perhaps drawing on their own perspectives, have variously described the impact of academy schools, substantial investments in capital to replace struggling schools, the impact of the Chartered London Teacher Scheme, the impact of Teach First, the impact of school-to-school support, the impact of the Challenge Advisers. The truth is that these debates are somewhat sterile. The London Challenge worked through the combination of elements in imaginative and flexible ways. There was an alchemy involved.

And this prompts two further reflections, both touched on in the contributions to this book. The first is about the transferability of lessons from the London Challenge. The London

Challenge has been theorised and can be seen in the context of approaches to system-wide reform. But because it was as much about the interaction of different elements, it is difficult to identify what 'should' be done in order to bring about the same sort of change in other urban areas. The London Challenge was extended by the 2005-2010 Labour government to Manchester and the Black Country, with positive results and Vanessa Ogden points out that since 2010 it has been extended to more rural areas, including Somerset and Norfolk. And something can be learnt from the London Challenge: the importance of addressing school failure, of championing success, of building frameworks for school-to-school support, of mobilising data. But systemic improvement is also contextual and copying from one context to another will never be wholly successful.

A second reflection relates to the longer term sustainability of area-based improvements. The principle of school-to-school support is not only established in London but has been used as a template for improvement across the country in what David Hargreaves has called a 'self-improving' system (Hargreaves, 2012). Ofsted (2010) cited the success of partnerships between schools as a key driver for success in London. The question for the future is whether these partnerships can continue to thrive without the policy framework provided by London Challenge. London schools remain successful – some of them, quite extraordinarily so. But urban school improvement is tough. Over time, as people move on, as new policy priorities arrive, it may prove difficult to sustain long-term momentum. Local relationships fray without the driving force of a Tim Brighouse or a David Woods. The long-term question for London is whether the moral drive for improvement alone can sustain a high-performance school system, and on that, only time will tell.

References
and Sources

**Oxford English
Dictionary
for Schools**

Ainscow, M. and West, M. (Eds.) (2006) *Improving Urban Schools: Leadership and Collaboration,* Maidenhead: Open University Press.

Ball, S. (2003) *Class Strategies And The Education Market: The Middle Classes And Social Advantage,* London: Routledge Falmer.

Bangs, J., MacBeath, J. and Galton, M. (2011) *Reinventing Schools, Reforming Teaching,* Abingdon: Routledge.

Barber, M. and Dann, R. (1996) *Raising Educational Standards In The Inner Cities: Practical Initiatives In Action,* London: Cassell.

Barber, M. and Mourshed, M. (2007) *How The World's Best Performing School Systems Come Out On Top,* London: McKinsey & Co.

Barlin, D and Hallgarten, J. (2001) *Supply Teachers: Symptom Of The Problems Or Part Of The Solution*, London: Institute of Public Policy Research.

Barnes, M. and Prior, D. (Eds.) (2009) *Subversive Citizens: Power, Agency And Resistance In Public Services,* Bristol: The Policy Press.

Brighouse, T.M. (2005) *'Remote Leadership'* in Coleman, M. and Earley, P. (Eds.) *Leadership And Management In Education: Cultures, Change And Context,* Oxford: Oxford University Press.

Brighouse, T.M. (2007) *'The London Challenge: A Personal View'* in Brighouse, T.M. and Fullick, L. (Eds.) *Education In A Global City: Essays From London,* London: Bedford Way Papers.

Brighouse, T.M. (2008) *'The Passionate Teacher And The Passionate Leader In The Passionate School'* in Davies, B. and Brighouse, T. (Eds.) *Passionate Leadership In Education,* London: Sage.

Brighouse, T.M. and Fullick, L. (2007) *The London Challenge Education In A Global City, London Institute Of Education.*

Brighouse, T.M. (2008) *Interview As 'The First Adviser'*, London, Institute of Education Magazine.

Brighouse, T.M. and Woods, D.C. (2008) *London Challenge School Improvement Butterflies*, DfES.

Brighouse, T.M. and Woods, D.C. (2013) *The A-Z of School Improvement, Principles and Practice*, Bloomsbury.

Brighouse, T.M. and Woods, D.C. (2008) *What Makes A Good School Now?*, Continuum.

Brighouse, T.M. and Woods, D.C. (2006) *Inspirations: A Collection Of Commentaries On School Improvement.*

Brighouse, T.M. (2012) *Essential Pieces: The Jigsaw Of A Successful School,* RM.

Brown, C., Husbands, C., and Woods, D.C. (2013) *Transforming Education For All: The Tower Hamlets Story,* London: London Borough of Tower Hamlets.

Bubb, S. and Earley, P. (2007) '*The School Workforce in London*' in Brighouse, T.M. and Fullick, L. (Eds.). (2007) *Education In A Global City: Essays From London,* London: Bedford Way Papers.

Bubb, S. & Earley, P. Nov (2007) *Education in a Global City: Essays on London.* Brighouse, T.M. & Fullick, L. (eds.). London: Institute of Education, University of London

Bubb, S. and Earley, P. (2007) *Leading And Managing Continuing Professional Development: Developing People, Developing Schools* (2nd edition), London: Sage.

Bubb, S. and Porritt, V. (2008) *Recognising And Developing Urban Teachers: Chartered London Teacher Status*, Management in Education, Vol 22, Issue 1, pp39-43.

Bush, A. (2005) *Choice And Equity In Teacher Supply*, London: Institute of Public Policy Research.

CfBT (2014) *Lesson From London Schools: Investigating The Success.*

CfBT (2014) *Lessons from London schools: investigating the success.* Reading: CfBT.

Clays, A., Kempton, J. and Paterson, C. (2014) *Regional Challenges: A Collaborative Approach To Improving Education.* London: Centre Forum.

Cockburn, A. and Haydn, T. (2004) *Recruiting And Retaining Teachers: Understanding Why Teachers Teach,* London, Routledge Falmer.

Day, C., Sammons, P., Leithwood, K., Hopkins, D., Gu, Q., Brown, E. and Ahtaridou, E. (2011) *Successful School Leadership: Linking Learning With Achievement*, Maidenhead: Open University Press.

Day, C., Stobart, G., Sammons, P., Kington, A., Gu, Q. and Mujtaba, T. (2006) *Variations In Teachers' Work, Lives And Effectiveness,* RR 743, London: DfES.

Department for Children, Schools and Families (2007) *Chartered London Teacher Status.*

Department for Children, Schools and Families (2008-2011) *Vision For London.*

Department for Children, Schools and Families (2008) *London Education On The Way To World Class.*

Department for Education (2010) *Lessons Learnt From London: Secondary School Improvement Programmes,* London: DfE.

Department for Education (2010) *The Importance of Teaching: The Schools White Paper,* London: DfE.

Department for Education and Skills (2002a) *The London Challenge.* Presentation February 2002.

Department for Education and Skills (2002b) *The London Challenge.* Presentation October 2002.

Department for Education and Skills (2003) *The London Challenge: Transforming London Secondary Schools,* Nottingham: DfES.

Department for Education and Skills (2005) *London Schools: Rising to the Challenge.*

Department for Education and Skills (2006) *London Challenge – From Good To Outstanding.*

Department for Education and Skills (annual publications between 2004-2010) *Families Of Schools.*

Department for Education and Skills (2003) *The London Challenge: Transforming London Secondary Schools.* London: DfES.

Department for Education and Skills (2004) *The London Challenge: Survey Of Pupils And Teachers,* Research Report 643, London: DfES.

Department for Education and Skills (2005) *Why Here? Report Of The Qualitative Work With Teachers Working In Schools Above And Below Floor Targets,* Research Report 666, London: DfES and IPPR.

Department for Education and Skills (2006) *School Workforce In England,* London: DfES.

Department for Education and Skills (2007a) *School Workforce In England*, London: DfES.

Department for Education and Skills (2007b) *Chartered London Teacher Guidance,* London: DfES.

Earl, L., Watson, N., and Katz, S., (2003) *Large-Scale Education Reform: Life Cycles And Implications For Sustainability,* London: CfBT.

Early, P., Weindling, D. and Crawford, M. (2005) *Evaluation Of The Leadership Strategy Of The London Challenge,* London Institute of Education.

Fullan, M. (2005) *'The Tri-Level Solution: School-District-State Synergy'* in *Education Analysis,* Winter, pp. 4-6, accessed at http://www.michaelfullan.ca/media/13396062320.pdf.

Fullan, M. (1999) *Change Forces: The Sequel*, London, Philadelphia: Falmer/ Routledge Press.

Fullan, M. (2001) *The New Meaning Of Educational Change*. Third Edition, New York: Routledge Falmer.

Fullan, M. Ed. (2009) *The Challenge Of Change: School Improvement Now!*, Thousand Oaks: Corwin.

Fullan, M. (2010) *All Systems Go: The Change Imperative For Whole System Reform*, Thousand Oaks: Corwin.

Fullan, M. (2011) *The Moral Imperative Realized*, Thousand Oaks: Corwin.

Fullan, M. and Boyle, A. (2014) *Big-City School Reforms: Lessons from New York, Toronto, and London*, Teachers College Press

Fullan, M. (2011) *Choosing The Wrong Drivers For Whole System Reform,* East Melbourne: Centre for Strategic Education.

Greater London Authority (2005) *Statistics Of Schools In London: Key Facts 2001-2005,* London: GLA.

Hall, P. (2007) *London Voices, London Lives*, Bristol: Policy Press.

Halpin, D. (2003) *Hope And Education: The Role Of The Utopian Imagination*, London: Routledge Falmer.

Hargreaves, A. and Shirley, D. (2009) *The Fourth Way: The Inspiring Future Of Educational Change,* Thousand Oaks: Corwin.

Hargreaves, D. H. and Hopkins, D. (1991) *The Empowered School: The Management And Practice Of Development Planning,* London: Cassell.

Hargreaves, D.H. (2012) *A Self-Improving School System: Towards Maturity,* Nottingham: NCSL.

Hargreaves, L., Cunningham, M., Hansen, A., McIntyre D., Oliver, C., and Pell, T. (2007) *The Status Of Teachers And The Teaching Profession: Views From Inside And Outside The Profession,* Research Report 831A, London: DfES.

Harris, A., Gunraj, J., James, S., Clarke, P. and Harris, B. (2006) *Improving Schools In Exceptionally Challenging Circumstances,* London: Continuum.

Her Majesty's Inspectorate (2003) *Schools' Use Of Temporary Teachers,* London: Government Printing Office.

Higham, R., Hopkins, D. and Matthews, P. (2009) *System Leadership In Practice,* Berkshire: Open University Press.

Higgins, S., Katsipataki, M., Kokotsaki, D., Coleman, R., Major, L. E. and Coe, R. (2013) *The Sutton Trust – Education Endowment Foundation Teaching and Learning Toolkit,* London: Education Endowment Foundation

Hill, R. (2012) *Teach First: The First 10 Years Of Impact,* London: Teach First.

Hopkins, D. (2007) *Every School A Great School,* Berkshire: Open University Press.

Hopkins, D. (2012) *'What Have We Learned From School Improvement About Taking Educational Reform To Scale?'* in Chapman, C., Armstrong, P., Harris, A., Muijs, D., Reynolds, D. and Sammons, P. (Eds.) *School Effectiveness And Improvement Research, Policy And Practice: Challenging The Orthodoxy?,* Abingdon: Routledge.

Hutchings, M., Greenwood, C., Hollingworth, S., Mansaray, A. and Rose, A. with Minty, S. and Glass, K. (2012) *Evaluation of the City Challenge Programme,* Institute of Policy Studies in Education, London Metropolitan University

Hutchings, M., Menter, I., Ross, A. and Thomson, D. (1999) *Teacher Supply And Retention Project,* Institute for Policy Studies in Education, University of North London.

Hutchings, M. (1999) *Teacher Supply And Retention In London 1998-1999*, Teacher Training Agency, University of North London.

Hutchings, M., Maylor, U., Mendick, H., Menter, I. and Smart, S. (2005) *An Evaluation Of Innovative Approaches To Teacher Training On The Teach First Programme*, London: IPSE.

Hutchings, M, Greenwood, C, Hollingworth, S, Mansaray, A and Rose, A (2012) *An evaluation of City Challenge*, London: IPSE.

Katwala, S. (Ed.) (2005) *Why Life Chances Matter: The Interim Report Of The Fabian Commission On Life Chances And Child Poverty*, London: Fabian Society.

Le Grand, J. (1995) *'Knights, Knaves Or Pawns? Human Behaviour And Social Policy'* in *The Journal Of Social Policy*, Vol. 26:2, p. 149-169.

Le Grand, J. (2007) *The Other Invisible Hand: Delivering Public Services Through Choice and Competition*, Woodstock: Princeton University Press.

Levin, B. (2008) *How To Change 5000 Schools*, Harvard: Harvard Educational Press.

Lipsky, M. (2010) *Street-Level Bureaucracy: Dilemmas Of The Individual In Public Services*, Thirtieth Anniversary Expanded Edition, New York: Russell Sage Foundation.

The London Leadership Strategy, (2008) *Portfolio Of Programmes.*

The London Leadership Strategy, (2008) *Reflections On The Journey From Good To Great.*

The London Leadership Strategy, (2011) *The Nine Pillars Of Greatness*, Pamphlet.

Lupton, R. (2006) *'How Does Place Affect Education?'* in Delorenzi, S. (Ed.) *Going Places: Neighbourhood Ethnicity And Social Mobility*, London: IPPR.

Lupton, R. and Sullivan, A. (2007) *'The London Context'* in Brighouse, T. and Fullick, L. (Eds.) *Education In A Global City: Essays From London*, London: Bedford Way Papers.

Matthews, P. and Sammons, P. (2006) *Supporting Leadership & Securing Quality: An Evaluation Of The Improvement Of The London Leadership Strategy*, NCSL.

Matthews, P. and McLaughlin, C. (2010) *Up For It, How Good Schools Become Great With A Little Help From Their Friends*, LLS.

Matthews, P. (2008) *Handbook For Local Leaders Of Education*, 2nd edition, National College for School Leadership, London Challenge.

Marshall, P. (Eds) (2013) *The Tail – How England's Schools Fail One Child In Five – And What Can Be Done*, Profile Books.

Mayor of London (2007) *The State Of London's Children*.

Mayor of London (2012) *The Mayor's Education Inquiry*.

McDermott, K.A. (2000) *Barriers To Large-Scale Success Of Models For Urban School Reform*, Educational Evaluation and Policy Analysis, Vol. 22, No. 1, pp. 83-89.

McNamara, O., Lewis, S. and Howson, J. (2004) *The Recruitment Of Otts*, Birmingham: NASUWT.

NFER (2011) *Evaluation Of City Challenge Leadership Strategies*.

Norris, E., Kidson, M., Douchal, P. and Rutter, J. (2014) *Doing Them Justice – Lessons From Four Case Studies Of Policy Implementation* (one of which is London Challenge), Institute for Government.

Ofsted (2010) *The London Challenge*, London: Ofsted.

Ofsted (2010) *Inspection Report On The London Challenge*.

Ofsted (2013) *Unseen Children: Access And Achievement 20 Years On*.

Ofsted (2006) *Improvements In London Schools 2000–2006*, www.ofsted.gov.uk.

Ogden, V. (2012) *Making Sense Of Policy In London Secondary Education: What Can Be Learned From The London Challenge?*, Doctoral Thesis, London: Institute of Education Library.

Payne, C.M. (2008) *So Much Reform, So Little Change: The Persistence Of Failure In Urban Schools*, Harvard: Harvard Educational Press.

Poet, H. and Kettlewell, K. (2011) *Evaluation Of City Challenge Leadership Strategies: London Area Report*, Slough: NFER.

Power, S., Edwards, T., Whitty, G. and Wigfall, V. (2003) *Education And The Middle Class*, Buckingham: Open University Press.

Preston, C. and Danby, M. (2005) *Who Are The Supply Teachers?*, London: MirandaNet & Select Education.

Sahlberg, P., (2012) *Finnish Lessons: What Can The World Learn From Educational Change In Finland?*, New York, Teachers College Press.

Sammons, P., Hillman, L. and Mortimore, P. (1995) *Key Characteristics Of Effective Schools: A Review Of School Effectiveness Research*, London: Institute of Education.

Save the Children (2011) *Severe Child Poverty, Nationally and Locally*, Briefing, February 2011, www.savethechildren.org.uk,

Smithers, A. and Robinson, P. (2005) *Teacher Turnover, Wastage And Movements Between Schools*, London: DfES.

Stobart, G. (2007) *Teachers' Work, Lives And Effectiveness Over Time – The VITAE Project*, INSI Research Matters No. 30, London, IoE.

Street, H. (2011) *Evaluation Of Primary Challenge Groups*, HLS Associates.

West, A. (2007) *'Poverty And Educational Achievement: Why Do Children From Low-Income Families Tend To Do Less Well At School?'* in Benefits Vol.15, No. 3: 283-297, London: The Policy Press.

West, A., Mattei, P. and Roberts, J. (2010) *'Accountability And Sanctions In English Schools'* in British Journal of Educational Studies Vol.59:1,p. 41-62, London: Routledge.

Whitty, G. (2002) *Making Sense Of Education Policy*, London: Paul Chapman Publishing.

Wilson, S., Benton, T., Scott, E. and Kendall, L. (2007) *London Challenge: Survey Of Pupils And Teachers 2006*, RR 823, London: DfES.

Woods, D.C. (2007) *Capital Gains: The London Challenge, Journal Of Improvement.*

Woods, D.C. and Macfarlane, R. (Eds.) (2010) *Going For Great*, LLS.

Woods, D.C. and Macfarlane, R. (Eds.) (2011) *Glimpses Of Greatness*, LLS.

Woods, D.C. and Macfarlane, R. (Eds.) (2012) *Growing Greatness*, LLS.

Woods, D.C. and Macfarlane, R. (Eds.) (2013) *Generating Greatness*, LLS.

Woods, D.C. and Macfarlane, R. (Eds.) (2014) *Gathering Greatness*, LLS.

Woods, D.C. and John, S. (Eds.) (2010) *Lesson Learned From London*, DCSF.

Wyness, G. (2011) *London Schooling: Lessons From The Capital,* Centre Forum.

Zavadsky, H. (2010) *Bringing School Reform To Scale: Five Award Winning Urban Districts,* Harvard: Harvard Educational Press.

"*Never doubt that a small group of thoughtful and committed citizens can change the world. Indeed, it is the only thing which ever has.***"**

Margaret Mead

Book design and photography by pandamedia.me